When

The

Vow

Breaks

When The Vow Breaks

RICHARD T. D'AVANZO
with Tim and Julie Canuteson

Pacific Press® Publishing Association
Nampa, Idaho
Oshawa, Ontario, Canada
www.pacificpress.com

Book design and cover photo by Steve Trapero

Copyright 2006 by
Pacific Press® Publishing Association
Printed in the United States of America

All the stories in this book are true. The names, locations, and unimportant characteristics of some of the individuals mentioned have been altered to protect their privacy. Any resemblance to people other than the author and his family is strictly coincidental.

ISBN: 0-8163-2138-8
ISBN 13: 9780816321384

Additional copies of this book are available by calling toll free 1-800-765-6955 or by visiting <http://www.adventistbookcenter.com>.

06 07 08 09 10 • 5 4 3 2 1

Dedication

To my wife, Maria,
and to the rest of my family—all of whom I love dearly

Contents

Introduction

A few years ago the idea of being an author was as unthinkable to me as was the idea of experiencing a divorce after more than thirty years of marriage, going back to graduate school, becoming a Christian counselor, presenting divorce recovery seminars, and teaching ministerial students and future Christian counselors—yet it has all happened. In this volume, I share my experience. I have focused upon the reaction of the human mind and spirit to God under the most distressing of circumstances. Because I wanted to focus upon the redemptive love of God for all parties involved, I have intentionally refrained from exploring church teachings regarding divorce and re-marriage.[1]

None of us comes across at our best amid the fires of a divorce. But I share my story, and inevitably in the telling, share the story of my family. I journaled our struggles during those difficult years, never thinking I would be sharing the experiences with you. Many times the powers of darkness tried to prevent me from writing this book. But the Lord overruled, I believe, because He wants to do for you what He's done for me. He wants to use your suffering to bring a wonderful good into your life even though you see no way you could experience such an outcome. I understand your skepticism; I was where you are.

---

[1]For more on this, see Appendix B: Seventh-day Adventist Church Standards on Divorce and Remarriage, a summary of the Adventist Church's teaching regarding these matters.

I am continually amazed that the lessons the Lord taught me during those dreadful times are absolutely pivotal for my happiness now! It was during my most painful times that I learned the most valuable lessons—those that keep me close to the Lord today. Don't let your pain be wasted. Allow it to lead you to the Lord Jesus so He may anchor your life in His awesome love, joy, and peace.

I've surrendered this book into the Lord's hands. Now it's in yours for your abundant blessings.

Part I:
My Story

CHAPTER 1

Beginnings

"Please, Claire," I begged through the bathroom door, "tell me what's the matter. Tell me what I'm doing wrong or what I can do so things can be better." The muffled sobs tore my heart out as I stood in the hallway of our Connecticut home. "Please tell me!" I said once more, pleading as earnestly as I could through the closed door, remembering her contorted face as she had rushed toward the bathroom before the tears overflowed.

"You should know what's wrong," her tear-choked voice replied.

I was honestly and completely baffled. I knew things were not all they should be, but I had never expected this. Claire and I had spent decades chasing the American dream and had achieved more than most. Yet, standing there in our dream home in the midst of our lakeside estate and surrounded by the trappings of success, I was no longer a successful businessman or philanthropist. In spite of all the social climbing I had done from my humble beginnings, I was touching bottom.

"Claire, what can I do to make things better?" I begged.

"You already know."

It was maddening for both of us. I didn't know, but she said I did. She knew but wouldn't tell.

"Please—" I tried again, but she cut me off.

"Just go away. Leave me alone!"

As I trudged down to the lakeshore to try to sort it all out, the beauty of the lake and the home we'd built seemed to mock me. How could the sun still shine when my world was falling apart? Later that night as I lay awake in bed with Claire's back turned toward me, I searched my life for clues but found none. How could this be happening? How could something so wonderful, so beautiful, so magical as the love we shared be going so wrong? My mind raced from scene to scene as my past seemed to rise up before me.

I meet Claire

The first pictures I saw were happy scenes of West Hartford, Connecticut, where I grew up. West Hartford was famous for the American School for the Deaf and for the fact that it was the birthplace of Noah Webster, but these things meant little to me. I do remember the colonial houses set on large lots shaded by giant oak trees, and my parents, who were warm and affectionate and who loved my two younger brothers and me dearly. My father, a strong, yet gentle Italian-American man, was haunted by pain—a strange shooting pain that passed from his mouth to his left eye. No one understood or seemed able to treat the pain he had to endure.

When I was thirteen, my parents decided to take my brothers and me on our first real family vacation. We were to spend three whole weeks at the beach in a rented cottage. I can't tell you how excited I was!

We arrived late one summer afternoon in Clinton, Connecticut, a typical seashore village flanked by a grand harbor. Gentle waves lapped the edges of the Long Island Sound, charming shops dotted the streets, and graceful flowerbeds lent their color and welcome to this little vacation haven. For me, the place was magical. *It's the perfect place for a boy to vacation,* I thought, as the sunlight turned the wavelets into sparkling diamonds so bright that looking at them hurt my eyes.

The ever-changing, ever-moving sea had me mesmerized—until I discovered another beautiful sight: the gorgeous blond girl who lived right across the street from me in another rented cottage. My boyish heart thumped excitedly as I whispered to myself, "She's beautiful!" However, my hormones had just begun to turn my attention from amateur radio, stamp collecting, and model trains to the opposite sex, and my almost painful shyness around girls threatened to keep me a silent observer.

In the morning, my family headed out to the beach, and we set up our chairs and blankets. I noticed the girl's family some distance away and longed to be closer. The next day, as luck would have it, we did move a little closer to them. And slowly, as the days went by, the distance between our families shrank. But I still didn't find the nerve to do more than gaze at the object of my affection.

Every evening, I dragged my younger brothers out to play ball on the grassy square separating our cottages, hoping against hope that she might pass by. Often she did, walking the family dogs. As I found out later, her parents were watching our activities with amusement, commenting that she never walked the dogs at home!

By the time two weeks had passed, our families' places on the beach were right next to each other. One day, I headed for the waves, beach ball in hand. At low tide, a person could walk out a considerable way before the water reached one's waist. There, in this watery world, I spotted my vision of loveliness, her shimmering blond hair tied back in a ponytail that hung gracefully down her back, contrasting with her tanned skin and maroon bikini. I threw her the ball, sensing instinctively that she would respond. Soon we were laughing, talking, and playing as though we had known each other forever. It must have been two hours before we came back to shore.

Our parents had noticed our time together, and they encouraged our friendship by becoming friendly themselves. The rest of the week flew by as Claire and I played constantly in the sand and sea.

Much to my delight, I discovered that Claire lived about fifteen miles from me. Excited by the prospect of visiting after our vacation ended, I took her phone number and address. But visiting turned out to be more work than I had realized. I had to get a map of the area before I could even plot my course. At last the great day arrived. I started out on my bike at 9 a.m. and arrived later in the morning, out of breath but exhilarated with my success. I felt at ease at Claire's home since I knew her parents from the beach. So, Claire and I talked comfortably while her mom made lunch for us.

This visit was the first of many over the following years, as we became integral parts of each other's lives. I decided that while girls were all right in general, this one was very special. I knew I loved her, but I couldn't come right out and say it for fear that she didn't feel the same about me. Eventually, I wrote her a letter in a mixture of English, French, and Morse code, thinking that she wouldn't bother to decode it unless she was truly interested in what I was saying. That way I'd find out how much she liked me without dying of embarrassment. I mailed my letter with great anticipation, but as time passed, my anticipation turned to dread. Finally, I could wait no longer, and I called her. She said she couldn't read my letter. I was crushed, but I tried not to show it. Then, a couple months later, she told me that she and a girlfriend had gone to the library and deciphered every word. Best of all, she liked it—and me!

Every summer our families continued to rent the same houses at the beach, and with each summer our affections grew. The second summer we held hands, and as her hand touched mine, I'm sure my feet left the ground. The next summer, we had our first kiss. By now, we were best of friends, and loving each other was easy. I was fifteen, and Claire was fourteen. As much as we cared about each other, our relationship never included the exclusivity of "going together." Somehow, we both understood that at our ages and with the distance between us, it was best that we see other people. So that's what we did, all the while reserving a special place in our hearts for each other.

A lot happened that year. For many years, I had seen my father deal with his pain by biting a folded towel and clenching his fists to keep from screaming out. His pain was almost certainly due to trigeminal neuralgia, which causes what medical literature calls the most terrible pain known to humankind. By the year I became fifteen, the pain had become so intense that my father decided to undergo an operation. The surgeon would cut the trigeminal nerve on the left side of his face, eliminating the sensations there—and thus, if successful, stopping his pain. We all hoped the surgery would work, but our hopes were tragically disappointed when my father died during the operation.

Life changed for me after my father died. I had to grow up quickly and take on new responsibilities in caring for my mother and my two younger brothers. My brothers and I moved into a room in the attic so Mom could rent out our bedrooms. That enabled her to keep the house and provide for us.

Dating other people

Claire and I both dated other people throughout high school and college. Our relationship was hard to pin down. We were like best friends, yet something more too. Whenever we were together, we just picked up where we left off. Adopted at two and a half by loving but undemonstrative parents, Claire looked to me as a stabilizing influence in her life. I was the one she called when she had a problem, even when it was with a boyfriend. We remained close for a while, but gradually lost touch as college progressed. Finally, I graduated and took a job as a stockbroker in Boston, ready to enter the vocational world and make something of myself.

Some years later, I bumped into Claire in a Boston restaurant. I was totally unprepared for the shock I felt when she introduced me to her fiancé. Learning that she was engaged stirred up all sorts of feelings inside me. I wanted to hate the guy and make him leave her alone, yet I had no right to claim her. Quite the opposite—I was there with a date too. So I contented myself by telling Claire in a private moment that this guy didn't look right for her. "Your date doesn't look like the right one for you either," she countered with a smile and slipped me her phone number.

We met casually at first, slipping easily back into the old habits of our friendship, treading lightly, unsure if there was still hope for us. One day she told me she had doubts about her fiancé. Wow, did I ever shift gears! When I realized there was a chance for me, I saw her daily, showering her with flowers and attention, determined not to let her go again. She had plans to go home to Connecticut one weekend, and I decided to go along since it was so close to my mother's home.

I'd known Claire's family almost as long as my own, and when they invited me for dinner at six that evening, I was glad to accept. I had no idea Claire had a date with her fiancé at nine, which would have explained some of the uneasiness in the house as that hour approached. Her parents made sure we knew that they liked me much better than they liked Claire's fiancé. Poor Claire was stuck with all kinds of emotions when she left for her date that evening. She couldn't have been much fun, although I'm sure her fiancé thought she was even less so a few days later, when she broke their engagement. I, however, was ecstatic!

After that, we were together constantly, and our love flourished. Claire was working as a private-duty nurse for a very wealthy family on a beautifully landscaped estate. I decided to meet her there after work one fall day and propose in that picturesque setting.

I was fairly certain that she'd say yes; still, I was a bundle of nerves as we walked the grounds. "Claire," I said, "we've been together for so many years. I can't imagine my life without you as a part of it. Will you marry me?"

The world seemed to stand still, and all nature listened for her answer. Then, amidst the rustle of dried leaves, the sweetest voice I'd ever known, the only voice I longed to hear, said Yes. My heart nearly leaped out of my chest as I gazed at the very vision of loveliness that had so caught my eye when I was only a boy of thirteen. Six months later I married the first girl I ever kissed, the one person I had loved longer than anyone outside my family.

Claire and I had enjoyed a storybook romance, and now married life opened before us like a wonderful new world. And we were eager for its challenges—both of us were ambitious for success. We started buying older properties, fixing them up, and renting and managing them on the side.

After eight years of this "second job," we had more than eighty rentals to manage, and I was exhausted. I said, "Claire, I've decided to quit my job and just do real estate full time."

She exploded. "How can you do that? What will happen to us?"

"Honey, I'm beat. I just can't do both jobs anymore. We'll be all right, really."

Claire wouldn't believe me, and that decision precipitated what was probably the worst—almost the only—fight of our married life up to that point. I found her reaction so surprising that I hardly knew what to say. Gradually it dawned on me that she felt her security threatened and nothing I could say would comfort her. In the months that followed, however, Claire relaxed as she saw that our income remained steady and then increased substantially as I purchased even more apartments. Once more, life settled into a familiar routine.

Just how long we would have continued our climb into the good life is hard to say because outside influences started demonstrating in the smallest of ways that our love was silently slipping away. In retrospect, I can see that there were signs and indications of problems long before the disease of neglect showed any open symptoms in our marriage. At first, vacations seemed to recharge our love, but the effect faded in a matter of days after we returned home.

Other interests

Gradually, we each found other interests to fill the emptiness. Claire returned to school, earning first a masters degree and then her doctorate, but her parents barely acknowledged her success. This fact grieved her deeply, adding another hurt to a private burden she was finding increasingly hard to bear. Only many years later did she learn from a mutual friend that her father had been proud of her and of what she had accomplished.

While Claire sought fulfillment in school, I too was changing, seeking deeper meaning in life than simply the acquisition of wealth. I found myself drawn to religion, often spending hours studying the Bible and other spiritual books. Twenty years of hard work and investing had brought us to a point where I didn't have to keep working just to earn a living.

Our solid financial position allowed both Claire and me to explore other humanitarian interests. We decided to sponsor a family unable to get out of the refugee camps in Southeast Asia and bring them to our home in America. Our efforts with the immigration bureaucracy were frustrating to the utmost. Quickly we decided that we could achieve much more if we flew to Bangkok, Thailand, and talked to immigration directly. So Claire and I made the first of what would become for me multiple trips to the refugee camps.

In the camps, I was confronted for the first time with human need brought down to its irreducible minimum. Seeing more than two hundred thousand people in such abject poverty and deplorable conditions was one of the most riveting experiences I've ever had. It affected my whole outlook on life and gave new meaning to my religious experience. These men, women, and children not only lacked food, shelter, and clothing, but they also lived with the horrible fear that nothing would ever change for them unless they were allowed to immigrate—which they knew was a near impossibility.

Over the next five years, I found myself not only spending many thousands of hours working in every way possible to give these people hope but also investing and raising many thousands of dollars. I found this experience so satisfying on so many levels that it would have seemed like a dream come true had not a greater vision taken its place. Couldn't we bring an orphaned refugee home with us and provide the child all the opportunity America has to offer? I didn't realize it at the time, but Claire agreed to this idea because she saw it as a way to find the kind of love and attention she had desired in our marriage.

After much difficulty with immigration, a thirteen-year-old girl arrived at our home in Connecticut. Unfortunately, the experience wasn't quite what Claire had hoped for. It is nearly impossible for one who hasn't been exposed to the horrors of war, to being torn from family and finally fleeing one's own country, to understand what traumas this beautiful Vietnamese girl had been through. The culture shock was incredible. She was so detached and bewildered that it was as if she had an iron band around her heart and couldn't give or receive love.

The wall she placed between herself and others was impenetrable. For nearly three weeks she didn't say a word—not one. We knew she could talk because we had heard her do so on our visits to the camps. I instinctively knew that the one thing her difficult life needed, the only thing that could open the door to her heart, was genuine love, and I was determined that she have it, even though at times she was difficult to love. And after about a year, love worked, and she eventually opened up and blossomed beautifully.

By the end of that year, we were able to add two Cambodian children to our home—a very cute thirteen-year-old girl and a remarkable nineteen-year-old boy. With our twenty-year-old biological son, who was very supportive of a larger family, we now had a family of six. While the older boys were in college, the girls kept us hopping at home. Yet I wouldn't trade the experience for anything! Being a proud father to my biological son and giving those children a home and a new life in America were some of the most enjoyable and meaningful experiences of my life. I continued returning to the refugee camps for about a month at a time for another three years, often stopping en route in Hawaii to vacation with Claire, who no longer went on the long trips to the camps. Still, all was not well—even in paradise.

Claire and I had made friends in Hawaii, and in the weeks we spent there, one of Claire's girlfriends saw in our marriage a reflection of her own discontented and troubled relationship. She planted some seeds that were to yield an ugly harvest. This woman was an active Christian, yet she decided my interest in religious matters was too strong. She told Claire, "People don't have to be that religious to be good Christians." She implied that I was fanatical, "over the edge"—just too enthusiastic and rigid about my beliefs. Inherent in the discussion was the implication that Claire might need to consider a future without me.

Certainly, I was different from the person I had been—someone whose main interest had been making money. Now I was more concerned with making the world a better place by serving God. Was I too religious? Perhaps from an outsider's perspective I was. Often, when someone finds a new love—be it a person, a sport, a hobby, or even God—that person tends in the beginning to allow the new interest to become all-consuming. But in time the new interest can mature and become more balanced.

I believe now that God gave me the experience in the refugee camps to broaden and deepen my love for all people, to make my religion practical and meaningful. At the time, I didn't think that my relationship with God kept me from loving my wife. In fact, I thought few things I had ever done provided such a great basis from which to love her. But Claire didn't seem to see it that way at all. In retrospect, I think she felt my good deeds and religious devotion were stealing my time and taking her place in my affections. I think my withdrawal from the traditional, work-a-day routine threatened her too. These feelings of discontent formed receptive soil for the seeds our friend planted about separation.

Visit to North Carolina

It wasn't long before Claire decided to act on those seeds. "I'm thinking of going down to North Carolina to drive around and check out the area. I just need to get away," she said.

I was taken aback, not because Claire didn't deserve some time away but because it was so out of character for her to want to head off on her own. The next day I urged her to let me go with her, and she agreed. We spent a couple of weeks traveling around there.

Then Claire said she was interested in buying a house in that particular area. I didn't understand that this was her way of saying she wanted a separation and was looking over this area with the intent to move there on her own.

Claire and I always seemed to have times of delicate rapprochement while on vacation, but we could never sustain it at home. Each time that we failed she felt rejected, and the wall of hurt she carried grew higher and still higher. By the time our kids were of age, there was no longer any way we could hide our troubles. If I tried to be affectionate, she turned away, and if I didn't try, she was hurt. Increasingly, she seemed to withdraw further and further away from me, while I couldn't imagine life without her.

At the dinner table one night, I could stand it no longer. There was silence between us— just the sounds of the silverware on the plates, the clatter of which aptly portrayed the discordant way we related to each other. "Claire, we've got to talk," I began. "Can we go into the library after dinner?" She nodded, and a few minutes later I settled into the sofa in this comfortable room with its cherry wood paneling, fireplace, and early American furniture.

"Claire, I don't even know where to begin," I started.

Then she took over the conversation. "Dick, there's no use in talking—my mind's made up. I'm divorcing you."

I couldn't believe my ears. In spite of all the problems we had experienced, I was always certain that somehow we'd make our marriage work. "How can you say that?" I asked incredulously.

23

She looked at me almost pityingly and sadly shook her head, "You should have known," she said. "You should have known."

"You've got to be kidding," I remonstrated, grasping at straws now.

"No, Dick, I'm serious. I am divorcing you."

I couldn't believe what I was hearing. In fact, from then on all I could hear was my own agony screaming from within. Life fell apart for me. I felt like I was in a whirling black hole. How would I ever survive? In the days, weeks, and months that followed, nothing made sense, and nothing seemed to work. My life was like a cartoon I saw once of two people arranging folding deck chairs on a cruise. One of the vacationers says, "Some people place their chair backwards so they can see where they've been, others face forward to see where they're going, and some people place theirs to see where they are right now. Which way are you going to place your chair?" The other replies, "I can't even get mine open!"

That was just how I felt. I didn't want to look forward because I saw no hope before me. I certainly didn't want to look back in despair. And I wouldn't have wished the place in which I found myself now on my worst enemy. I was simply too crushed, too disoriented, too hurt to look at the present with any kind of objectivity. If you could have looked inside my heart, you would have seen something resembling Humpty Dumpty after his great fall. I'd been shattered by the pain of rejection, the feelings of hopelessness, helplessness, and utter loneliness that result when the life one has built and thought he understood has been wrenched away. It's a living death. And like Humpty Dumpty in the nursery rhyme, all the king's counselors, psychologists, therapists, and psychiatrists couldn't put me back together again.

I sank deep into the despair of brokenness. Happiness meant recovering that which was impossible to regain, and in its absence, I knew that I could never be happy again. The years before me seemed to stretch endlessly away—all lonely, all sad, nothing to look forward to but the relief death would bring.

I remember praying to God and finding no relief, no comfort, no great revelation or cosmic experience—just the memory of a familiar verse from the twenty-third psalm: "Yea, though I walk through the valley of the shadow of death, I will fear no evil: for thou art with me" (KJV). Then I realized that if David could go through the valley of the shadow of death, perhaps there was a way I could survive as well, and a glimmer of hope was kindled in my heart. However, that hope faded as quickly as it came. Later, another glimmer shone in—only to fade away too. This process repeated itself over and over. In time, I realized that through this process, God was making Himself known to me and teaching me to walk with Him. He was using the pain and despair of divorce to draw me closer to Him.

Now, after conducting more than two hundred divorce recovery seminars, I can say authoritatively that countless others are finding that God not only can but is doing the same with them. No one can give you what you truly need for full recovery, no matter how many letters and degrees in counseling they may have after their name. Only God, who loves you dearly, can perform this miracle, and He is awaiting only your decision to walk with Him in the valley.

In my divorce, I saw only pain, despair, and loneliness, but God saw an opportunity. Let me share that story with you.

CHAPTER 2

"Hand, Hand"

After reading about my years dating Claire, you may be asking the same thing I found myself asking: How could something so wonderful turn out so horribly? I see now what my blind denial would not, could not, in spite of every evidence to the contrary, admit—our relationship died of neglect. Even up to the point when Claire told me she wanted a divorce, we hadn't had huge screaming fights or any of the other things one associates with failing marriages. Instead, we continued through the normal patterns of life.

However, when the estrangement that had been growing slowly and insidiously through the years became not just a matter of individual perceptions but also an acknowledged fact, I determined to alter that fact even at that late date. I just couldn't accept the death of my marriage, so I began to try to demonstrate my love in actions much more than I ever had in the past. I was in denial—the first stage of grief. I didn't realize it at the time, and because I didn't, I made a number of mistakes that must have driven Claire wild.

As Christmas approached, I pleaded, "Where can I start the rebuilding process? On what ground are you willing to start? Anywhere, Claire; I'll start anywhere. Please!"

Claire considered me silently. Then her eyes misted and deep, deep hurt washed over her features. "Dick, I don't think I could ever change my feelings. I've been hurt too much for too long."

"Does that mean there is no use in my trying?"

"Yes, it won't change anything."

"How can you do this to us? To hear you say there is no hope is crushing me. It's unbearable; it's throwing away thirty years—our family, our home, our future, and our family's future. Nothing that happened in the past should command such destructive power that it can rob us of our future. How can you do this?"

Claire shook her head and turned to leave, knowing further discussion was useless. "I'll always have hope for us," I said forlornly as she walked away.

So began the holiday season, and with it, fresh reminders of all I hadn't done. Claire wrote me a note. "Even with Christmas," it said, "you cannot see the unfairness of my having to decorate, shop, wrap, plan, cook, send out the cards, etc., etc., etc. I am a thousand times busier than you are, but do you care? The answer is clear every year—NO!"

What could I say? There was an element of truth in what she was saying. But there was more to it. Little hurts had stuck with her until they had grown into a painful wound that required only the slightest touch to bring all the agony to the surface, as if I had struck the wound intentionally.

Justifying divorce

Some days later found us feeling more comfortable with each other again, and the subject of my cousin's failing marriage came up as we worked together doing chores around the house. Impulsively, I hugged Claire and told her of my commitment to our marriage and family. She didn't push me away, but she let me know that as far as she was concerned, if people aren't happy or getting the love they need, then divorce is perfectly justified.

A chill ran down my spine that had nothing to do with the weather—as if the cold hand of death had reached out and grasped my marriage. I shook off the feeling and determined to show her even more clearly that I loved her. On Friday, I drove to the deli and picked up the cheesecake for her university function. After my Vietnamese daughter, Tina, helped me take the sheets I had washed earlier and remake our bed, I placed an "I love you" note under Claire's pillow. Then I ran out to pick up our Cambodian daughter, Pam, at the library so Claire wouldn't have to rush to meet her. The next day I straightened the living room before taking Claire to dinner and a stage play. She made my heart sing when she casually said, "I had a good time."

Motivated, I started the new week by wiping down the cellar stairs and vacuuming the cellar. Monday, I cleaned the stairs to the second floor and bought all the stocking stuffers for Christmas and then did the grocery shopping. Tuesday, I dusted and helped Tina with her college applications. Day after day I continued this pattern, seeking each and every opportunity to demonstrate my love for my wife. Little did I realize that in my refusal to accept the death of our marriage, I was driving the nails in the coffin of its demise, strengthening her conviction that I had never and would never understand her or be the soul mate for whom she longed. She was the reason for all my attempts at saving the marriage, and my actions were the admission of my failings, her final reason to seek a divorce.

During the next two years we continued this strange dance of my attempts at reconciliation and her movement further toward dissolving our union. It was a slow, agonizing process in which she would take two steps toward divorce and then one back. And every tiny step back toward me just encouraged the illusion that maybe, just maybe, I wouldn't have to face my greatest fear—that of being left totally and utterly alone.

I didn't know it, couldn't know it, but God was using this crisis in my life to reach out to me in a special way. I knew that He hadn't caused my problems, yet I also realized that He had allowed them to come upon me. "Why, God? *Why?* Please tell me why," I pled over and over. I couldn't see how this miserable divorce could have any positive effect upon me.

I prayed earnestly but found no quick fix, no immediate relief. I had read the Bible for years. It was a guide I trusted; in its pages I had found many precious truths. Now it seemed like a different book, less easily understood. It didn't seem to speak to my specific needs. Yet as I read, I caught a glimmer of hope. In Psalm 46:10, God told me, "Be still, and know that I am God" (KJV). When I read that verse, I felt like God was talking right to me, and emotions welled up inside me as I began to realize the full import of His Word. It was as if God Himself had placed a strong, but kind arm around me and had drawn me close beside Him as a loving father would draw his son. I felt that God was patiently explaining that He knew everything I was going through and that He could carry me through.

In the first verse of the same chapter I read, "God is our refuge and strength, an ever present help in trouble" (KJV)—only I read the verse as if God were talking to me personally, which is how it felt just then. I remembered the words of Psalm 23:4, "Yea, though I walk through the valley of the shadow of death, I will fear no evil: for thou art with me" (KJV). As I considered this awful valley and tried to understand practically what it meant for me at this point in my life, a new thought flashed into my mind—a suggestion that perhaps had divine origin. I visualized a huge truck that sped towards me and then bore off at the last moment, just missing me. Only its shadow passed over me. The breeze of this moving specter of death rocked me and the fear of death left me traumatized, yet I wasn't physically hurt.

Then I understood. Divorce is just like that truck. It comes at us threatening destruction, yet it is only the valley of the shadow of death that we are passing through, though it feels much worse. Through my experience both during and after my divorce, the Lord taught me how vital love and security are to all of us, no matter what our age. Take these away, and we agonize terribly. God used the pain and despair of my divorce to teach me to trust Him by placing my hand in His, and He desires to do the same for you. Pain is the common denominator in divorce: everyone loses. Yet if we are willing, God will use this bitter experience to draw us to Him so He may become a very real companion to us—One who will never leave or forsake us.

Reaching for a hand

Not long ago, God used my twenty-month-old granddaughter Amy to remind me again of this lesson. Amy's parents had to make a trip to New York City to attend meetings not suitable for a little girl, and they enlisted me to baby-sit every evening. Amy managed fairly well the first two nights, but Sunday afternoon real distress signs began to appear. She constantly wanted to know why Mommy and Daddy weren't home. I explained that they would be home late the next day, but such was her distress that my reassurances lasted only a few minutes and then I had to repeat them.

By the time I had completed the normal bedtime routine and placed Amy in her crib, she had lost it. She was in a complete panic. Mommy and Daddy had left her, and her world was crumbling down. I had put her to bed often when her parents went out for an evening, and never before had I witnessed such a reaction. To her little mind, two days without the love and assurance of her parents was forever, and she felt totally abandoned. As I put her in her crib, she screamed, "No, Papa. Mommy! Daddy!" It was her way of saying, "I don't understand. Mommy and Daddy are my love and my security. Where are they? I can't live without them!"

I hugged Amy tightly until she calmed down, and then I placed her gently in her crib, promising I wouldn't leave her. I left the railing down and stayed there, kneeling by the crib, my arm hanging loosely over the rail, my hand close to her. She hugged her bottle and stared blankly into space as tears slid silently down her cheeks. Once in a while she'd glance over toward me as if reassuring herself of my presence. Finally her breathing quieted and the tears stopped, but the blank stare continued through half-closed eyes.

Then came an unforgettable moment. Amy slowly reached out her hand and touched mine ever so gently. Her hand lingered just a moment and then moved away. Then it came back again and again and again, staying longer each time. After a half hour or more, she placed her hand permanently in mine. No words were spoken and none were needed. In that dark room we had communicated in the silent language of love.

I remembered how falteringly I had reached out to God in the darkness of my despair. I had considered myself a Christian for many years. In the Bible, I had seen truths that I could follow and the pathway God desires all of us to walk. In fact, it was in part my zeal for the truths of God's Word that had driven my wife and me apart. However, in spite of all my knowledge about God, I didn't know Him as I could have known Him. In my moment of crisis, I wondered how He could save me from the circumstances in which I found myself.

Like Amy, I reached out for God's extended hand and then pulled back. But the pain and emptiness remained. So I reached out again and again, until at last I found comfort there. Not what I wanted, not always in the way I wanted it, but God spoke to me, comforted me, and made me understand that I was loved at a time when I felt unloved and unlovable. Recalling this, I was overwhelmed with empathy for little Amy, and tears filled my eyes at the thought of the feelings of loneliness and emptiness that she must have. At last, she drifted off to sleep.

The next night, Amy's bedtime arrived before her parents did. She began to go through the same panic, but this time she stopped crying, held my hand, and went to sleep in just a few minutes. Since then, whenever Amy is the slightest bit upset, afraid, or insecure, she says to her parents or me, "Hand, hand."

The next several chapters tell how, through the pain of my divorce, I learned to put my hand in God's hand. It's a story of how God heals the pain that we think can't possibly be healed.

Are you hurting? You, too, can find the solution I did. It won't be easy, and right now you may feel too disoriented and crushed to even think about ever being happy again. Yet it can happen for you just as it did for me. Maybe, just maybe, I can share a few things that will help you on your journey.

CHAPTER 3

The Valley of the Shadow

I started seeing a Christian counselor. He could work only with my perspective, because Claire refused to talk with him. Nevertheless, he helped me to understand several things I might have missed without his objective views. He pointed out that Claire and I had gotten along reasonably well for the first twenty years of our marriage. However, as we began to look at Christianity in a serious way, I had responded more intensely than Claire had, which caused her to feel she was being replaced because she wasn't keeping up. In her mind, my zeal for God was a betrayal. She never verbalized this, and I, oblivious and insensitive to her fears, confirmed in her mind the very worst fear and insecurity— that her one and only had a new love.

That's ridiculous! I thought. *Christianity has only made me better able to love her.* Regardless of what I thought, however, my counselor felt that Claire had harbored these feelings, and as she did so, they slowly ate away at our relationship. My counselor believed that Claire had become convinced that I would never change, never meet her real needs, and never be the kind of person I used to be. He added that by the time I was aware we were in trouble—unfortunately, I had remained blissfully unaware that anything significant was happening—she had shut down any feelings toward me. Consequently, no matter what I did, it was too late to budge her from what she believed to be her only option—divorce.

Despite this objective assessment from a professional counselor, I desperately wanted to rescue my marriage from destruction. I wanted so badly to save my marriage that I didn't even realize I was in denial. Yet when I look back, I can clearly see that I was. I didn't understand it at the time, but I was entering into the stages of grief one experiences at a major loss. The reality of what was happening to me slowly began to sink in.

On my father's birthday, I wrote him a letter: "As you might know, Dad, Claire is divorcing me, and it has been so hard for me to lose the only one I have loved for thirty-five years—the one meant to be for the rest of my life. Sometimes the pain of it all, of seeing the effect upon the whole family as well as my own personal pain, seems unbearable. I have no choice but to go on with what remains of my life. . . . Perhaps when grandchildren come, they can bring meaning and joy— but it could never be to the degree it could have been with Claire. You left too soon, Dad; you left too soon. I miss you terribly. I sure would have liked you being beside me right now."

In my letter to my father, I reached out longingly for someone to go through this experience with me, to hold my hand and to comfort me. I was so hurt, so utterly alone even in my own home. This was not something I could fully share with my children. They had their own pains and struggles from our dissolving marriage and family. It would be absolutely unfair to add all my emotional needs to their burdens, even though they were all wonderful in this crisis. Gradually, it dawned on me that if I was to gain the necessary mental and emotional buttressing to get through this horrible experience, I had to cling to my heavenly Father's hand.

Weekends were terribly long and lonely. When I told God I didn't know how I could survive them, I got a call from Mark, an old friend. I told him how bad things were, and when he heard my plight, he said, "Well, let's spend the day at the beach."

"Great!" I said. "I'll pack a lunch."

We had a wonderful time. So, that summer, we spent every week-end at the beach. It was so refreshing to be out in nature with God and a loyal friend. We both came back recharged for another week.

Every time I put my hand in God's hand, He met my need. Sometimes He just gave me peace in my heart, and other times He had someone call me at just the right moment. But something always happened; God always answered—even if I didn't realize it at the time.

Learning to trust

When we walk with God, we discover our true spiritual condition. I had considered myself a Christian not just in name but in experience too. I had used my skills and my funds to effect changes for the better in people's lives, and I was pleased with the person I was. Now I was taking a good hard look in the mirror, and I wasn't enjoying what I saw. Even though I didn't see the insensitive monster that Claire, in her pain, apparently saw, neither did I see the man I had thought I was. In place of the self-confident man engaged in humanitarian activities, in place of the spiritual man leading out in Bible studies, in place of the businessman devoting his skill and knowledge to community and church, I saw only the tortured soul of a broken man who had gone to his spiritual well in need of refreshment and found it empty. My pride and arrogance were humbled, preparing me to learn the lessons God couldn't teach me during the good times. For the first time in my life I was really touching bottom, desperately looking to fill the empty void my life had become. I knew all about God, but I had yet to trust in Him completely.

I realized that in Claire's complaints there was an element of bitter truth. You see, all of us, unless submitted to a power outside ourselves, are self-serving. This is our very nature, and it finds expression in many, many ways. And perhaps in no other human relationship does it flourish quite as well as in marriage. Our most loving and considerate actions are all too often tainted with the unspoken idea of the quid pro quo: I do this for her, and she'll do that for me. Even in disagreements you can see this tit-for-tat type of game played back and forth. In counseling sessions, I hear men say things such as, "Well, if she hadn't yelled at me, I wouldn't have yelled at her." This is conditional love. "I'll love you as long as you are meeting my needs of the moment. But woe unto you if you fail to meet my needs." Oh, we don't say it quite like this, but our actions and our mannerisms display this attitude as clearly as if we had stated it plainly.

How do we begin to act contrary to the nature that draws us into self-centered behavior as naturally as we breathe? Fortunately, God promises that we can exchange our present heart for a new one that packages our desires and inclinations in a godly, selfless love. " 'I will give you a new heart and put a new spirit in you; I will remove from you your heart of stone and give you a heart of flesh. And I will put my Spirit in you and move you to follow my decrees and be careful to keep my laws' " (Ezekiel 36:26, 27).

"Well, Lord, if You can change me and give me a new heart, then do it now. And while You're at it, give one to Claire too!" That was my response. The problem was that I didn't understand how to obtain what I desired. I thought that if God put a new heart in me, I would feel better. Instead, I was going to have to learn to obtain this new heart in the way nearly every other human who has ever gained this experience has—in the school of suffering. Speaking of Christ, the Bible says, "Although he was a son, he learned obedience from what he suffered" (Hebrews 5:8). That's right! Obedience, walking in godly love, is learned behavior, and God often uses our suffering to teach it to us. God didn't cause my divorce, but He used the opportunity it presented to reach into my heart in a new and deeper way.

No matter what our experience, there are defects in our character and impurities in our soul that God desires to remove. The problem is that to examine—let alone remove—such things is painful. Yet it is in the fires of our painful affliction that God will do His mighty work in us if we're willing. In fact, the greatest thing God ever did was done through pain—the crucifixion of His Son, Jesus, which provided our salvation. Nevertheless, few there are among us who willingly embrace pain. So,

God patiently waits until circumstances make us so uncomfortable that we're willing to put our hand in His in order to grow and learn. This is not something we naturally seek out, and when it comes upon us, it is often the last thing in the world that we desire. Yet if we face and grasp the opportunity, we can experience wonderful changes.

The Bible is replete with examples of such situations. Joseph had no idea when he set out to visit his brothers that they would sell him into slavery. David had no concept of the trouble that was coming his way as a result of the prophet Samuel's anointing him. Likewise, when King Nebuchadnezzar began to erect a golden image, Daniel's three friends had no idea that it would put a severe strain upon their loyalties. Praise God, when they were offered the choice of being burnt alive or yielding principle, they were willing to suffer! And God sustained them in the fires of affliction. In fact, it was their being thrown in the fire that revealed His power. God desires to reveal His power in our lives amid the conflicts we face in divorce. He wants to say, "Behold, I have refined you, but not as silver; I have tried and chosen you in the furnace of affliction" (Isaiah 48:10, Amplified).

Here's what God wants to come out of the furnace of affliction in which we find ourselves: gold refined in the fire until all the impurities are burned away and only the lustrous pure metal remains. The process takes time, but know with certainty that the very fact that you are facing such a situation is evidence that God is using it to draw you to Him, for He never allows anything into our experience except that which He wants to use for our eternal benefit. The key is for us to be willing to trust Him and accept His refining so our pain and anguish isn't wasted.

"How long, Lord?"

Unfortunately, such objectivity does not come easily in the flames of divorce. I read, "Humble yourselves therefore, under God's mighty hand, that he may lift you up in due time" (1 Peter 5:6). I felt I had been humbled, and I couldn't wait to have God lift me up, so I found myself pleading, "How long, Lord? How long?" The only reply I got was right in the verse itself: "in due time." This wasn't very satisfying, and I read further until I found a verse that told me this would happen "after you have suffered a little while" (1 Peter 5:10).

I said, "I'm not trying to be picky, Lord, but how long is 'a little while'?"

He replied, "You're going to have to trust Me. I can sustain you in your suffering, and I won't ever allow you to suffer any longer than is necessary to draw you closer to Me so that self is crucified and I live in its place. I'm the only One who knows when the time is right to bring you out of the valley of sorrow and pain. Dick, this is a taste of the bitter cup of sorrow. Right now it seems like the worst thing that could ever happen to you. But if you're willing to allow Me to work in your life, I can take this opportunity to prepare the way for a happiness beyond what you have ever known.

"When a woman is in labor, she can accept what is happening to her and go along with the painful transformation that prepares her body to give birth, or she can exhaust herself fighting against what must happen and even despair over her lot in life. In the end, she'll continue to be a woman in labor until either the work is finished or she perishes in the crisis. David said, 'If your law had not been my delight, I would have perished in my affliction' (Psalm 119:92). It was through submission to Me that David survived the years of conflict and peril. I want to protect and guide you as I did him."

I thought about David—driven from his home and his wife, hunted like a wild animal, betrayed at every turn, even by those who should have stood with him—and I realized there are parallels between his experience and that of every person involved in or considering a divorce. My situation hadn't gotten quite as bad as David's; nevertheless, I felt I, too, was perishing in my affliction. I decided I could try to trust God. After all, things couldn't get any worse, could they?

They did.

One night as Claire and I lay in bed, I sensed she was awake, so I began to talk to her in the dark, sharing the pain I had been going through. Although she made no response, the floodgates of my soul were open, and I couldn't stop the flow. I talked for about a half hour. Claire and I had shared all of life's burdens and disappointments, joys and victories, and now it seemed natural to share the pain caused by the death of our relationship. Perhaps that night Claire was wrapped in her own silent blanket of pain. All I know is that she seemed like a stranger. I spent the rest of the night in sleeplessness.

The next day Claire related my nighttime talk to her counselor, but she focused on her perception that I was about to commit suicide. This prompted Claire and her counselor to get me involved in psychiatric sessions right away. I felt that Claire had overreacted to my comments that night, and my pain rose to even greater heights when I realized I could no longer trust even my feelings to her—the one whom, up to that moment, I had trusted more than any other, perhaps even God.

It was then that I began to realize that God had been seeking to prepare me for what was coming. I came to understand that in spite of my desires, the journey I was on through divorce—through the valley of the shadow of death—was going to be more important to me than my goal of getting out of the valley. I was very slowly learning not to beg God to free me from my pain and suffering but to help me bear it more like Jesus would.

In my mind's eye, I pictured all the millions forced to enter this valley. The vast majority just huddle at the edge until they can somehow escape their dreadful valley, believing they have survived. Yet, they remain in the same condition in which they entered it, albeit perhaps more traumatized. Because they haven't allowed God to walk with them through their pain and haven't gained the lessons He could have taught them, they are very likely to find themselves repeating their journey over the same difficult ground. The only ones who come out having gained immeasurably from their experience are those who are willing to allow God to lead them. God takes those who follow Him on a journey of discovery and transformation deeper and still deeper into this dreadful valley until they have learned what it is to die to self and depend only upon a sovereign God of love. They exit on the other side very different from what they were when they entered it. And when they exit the valley, it has become ground they have allowed God to conquer through them. Then they're prepared to set off with God into a new and brighter future.

Realizing this, I slowly began to let God take me deeper into the valley of the shadow of death, not knowing just how deep and painful such a death could be. I only knew that somehow I was going to have to trust God and not myself as I traveled through it. It was dawning on me that I wasn't going to find any pain-free way through divorce, and that while it wasn't a literal death, it was going to feel just as bad. With or without God, my experience was going to be painful. But with God, it would be painful only for a while and then I would find a life of prospering with more of God's love, joy, peace, and security than I had ever known.

"Only friends"

The valley deepened when Claire filed the legal papers for the divorce. "I only want to be friends and not be married anymore," Claire told me. I had feared this action more than anything else, and the agony it caused ripped through my heart. It left me angry and very depressed. My life seemed over.

Then God spoke to my heart. "Why are you so upset and hurt, Dick?" He said.

"Why? You know why, Lord. I have never suffered more distress in all my life than the pain of what I am going through right now, and You ask me 'why'?"

"Yes. I ask you, My son, because you said you were willing to give up your old ways of responding and to die to self in exchange for learning My ways of responding. Remember Galatians 2:20, which you taught to the Bible study class: ' "I have been crucified with Christ and I no longer live, but Christ lives in me.' " Dick, you're believing in what you think will be the outcome of your circumstances rather than trusting the outcome to Me. You think of going through the divorce as death. But by surrendering self to Me, the outcome of the death you see will be only a 'shadow' of death. Can a shadow harm you?"

"No, Lord."

"Then why are you letting Claire's actions and words have such an effect on you?"

"Perhaps it's because I have never really died to self, never really entered into this experience of trusting my present and future totally to You. At this point, I'm so drained that I'm not sure I really can!"

"I'll never force you. I love you with an everlasting love and will give only the very best for you. You'll find an underlying peace and internal joy even in the midst of this personal disaster if you surrender your emotions, will, and intellect to Me. It won't be easy, but the choice is yours."

It was hard to fight this kind of love and gentle logic, which never forced me and sought only my happiness and long-term good. Through my utter pain, I saw that I was fighting the greatest battle of my life— that of yielding self to God. I knew the only sensible way was to trust Him, even if I didn't like what appeared to be happening to me.

"Lord," I said, "now I'm willing to enter this experience with You. To be honest, I don't see how anything could be any worse than what is going on in my life. But while I can mentally choose to give up self to You with all its emotions of hurt, anger, frustration, fear, loneliness, and self-pity, these emotions and old ways of behaving are still overpowering me. How do I deal with them?"

"You surrender them to Me every time they try to rise and control you."

"But how do I surrender them to You?"

"Believe that I take them when you give them to Me even if you don't feel different. Then diligently focus on behaving like Jesus rather than focusing on the hurts and circumstances. As you do this, the presence of My peace in you will give you evidence that I am taking them from you. This peace will assure you that I will carry you through.

"And no matter what, you must remember to remain focused on meeting each frustration with the spirit of love, patience, and kindness that I've given you. This will be a hard task, for your natural inclination is to allow your emotions to dominate. Remember, dying to self means no longer trusting your emotions and even your intellect and will. Instead, it means trusting in My presence to enable you to behave as My child through it all."

I tried this and found it to be very reassuring. I wasn't perfect at it; many times I slipped back into old habits. But when I cooperated with God and stopped focusing on my turbulent emotions and old ways of seeing things and focused instead on being His child, I soon experienced a magnificent peace deep within—something that I had thought was gone from my life forever.

However, my experience of this peace often wasn't very long lasting because I was easily sidetracked. One such time was my first birthday after Claire decided she wanted a divorce. Birthdays were always a big deal in our family, but this one came and went without any recognition from her. No card, no present, not even a word. It hurt terribly. I was an emotional basket case. It was a little thing, one I should have anticipated, but my old ways of responding jumped back into control.

My old nature sneaked in and overpowered my commitment to let go of my old ways and to accept and trust my Savior, who loved me still and wanted to help me. I wallowed for a while in the agonies of those who know not a living God as an ever-present help in trouble. But God didn't discard me. Eventually He got through to me and pointed out that I had embraced the old way of life once more, and with it, all of its overpowering emotions of pain and suffering. "There is nothing good in trusting your old self, Dick. It must regularly be put to death so I can give you a new self that responds to My Spirit."

What about self-confidence?

I was seeing a couple of counselors, and about this time, they were contradicting what I believed God was teaching me, so I confronted God. "Lord, the counselors say I need a positive self-image and that I shouldn't tear myself down because this won't build self-confidence."

"Think about what they're telling you, Dick. Is your strength sufficient to sustain you when your emotions are out of control?"

"No."

"If self is that weak, Dick, why would you want to have any confidence in it? Your worst enemy isn't the trials you face, nor Claire, nor the legal proceedings. It's self. Serving self—whether it be with your intellect, desires, or emotions—is what separates you from the transforming effect of My presence in you. My love, joy, peace, patience, kindness, goodness, faithfulness, gentleness, and self-control all go out the window when you serve self. Gentleness and self-control must replace your old self-centeredness."

Jesus said it so simply, " 'If anyone wishes to come after Me, let him deny himself, and take up his cross daily, and follow Me' " (Luke 9:23, NAS). And as the apostle Paul penned, "We should not trust in ourselves, but in God" (2 Corinthians 1:9, NAS). I was finally beginning to understand what the Lord was trying to teach me. I had glimpsed the concept that my trials and sufferings were only tools to bring me closer to God. If I allowed it, my suffering would become God's catalyst to put my arrogant self to death.

I thought again of Paul, who wrote, "I delight in weaknesses, in insults, in hardships, in persecutions, in difficulties. For when I am weak, then I am strong" (2 Corinthians 12:10). Perhaps God inspired him to pass on this gem of hard-won wisdom because God knew that these many years later you and I would need a vision, a lofty goal, a paradox to make all we are going through—the pain we are suffering, the losses we feel—meaningful in the light of eternity and by the testimony of one who has trod the path of suffering before us. God assures us, " 'I will strengthen you and help you; I will uphold you with my righteous right hand' " (Isaiah 41:10).

Yes, I was beginning to understand why God invites all who are weary and burdened to come unto Him that they might find rest for their souls. Suffering is not God's plan for His children, but He has prepared a way of escape. Throughout history there have been those who, in times of bitterest sorrow, chose to go to a compassionate Savior to be rescued and transformed. The apostle Paul experienced it, and thousands upon thousands of others have as well. We can too, if we'll come to God and allow Him to change our hearts and remove the unworthy feelings and destructive behaviors that bring us such misery.

Remember, it's not our circumstances, no matter how bleak, that make us happy or sad. It's our reaction to them. God told us through Paul to be content whatever the circumstances (see Philippians 4:11, 12). This sounds impossible until we remember that the one who wrote this was himself repeatedly stoned, beaten, and imprisoned. In verse 13, he explains how we, too, can be content in our adversity: "I can do everything through him who gives me strength."

Paul understood that God was sovereign in his life and that even if he didn't enjoy or understand what was happening to him, he could trust God to use the circumstances for good. He was content by faith because he was anticipating the good he knew was in the making although still unseen. Thus he could say that he was always "giving thanks to God the Father for everything" (Ephesians 5:20). And he encouraged us to follow the same course: "Give thanks in all circumstances, for this is God's will for you" (1 Thessalonians 5:18).

It was a hard but vital lesson for me. Yet amid the struggle of giving up my ways and dying to self, I sensed God's sweet voice calling out to me in love, assuring me that everything would eventually be all right. I didn't know when He was going to deliver me out of this, but deep down I knew He would. " 'The Lord himself goes before you and will be with you; he will never leave you nor forsake you. Do not be afraid; do not be discouraged' "; " 'I have loved you with an everlasting love; I have drawn you with loving-kindness' " (Deuteronomy 31:8; Jeremiah 31:3).

CHAPTER 4

Dealing With Anger

"Lord, please help me never forget that You are allowing all that occurs to me. Teach me to treat all of this with the peace, trust, and faith that You give. Help me to surrender myself into Your loving control. You have allowed the circumstances I face for the refining and purging process, to sweep away the dross of my life, allowing me to serve You better. You put everything in my life, especially Claire. I see but dimly at times that the dying of self is preparing the way for me to be used in Your service."

So reads my journal entry written nine months after Claire filed for divorce. Perhaps all those who have ever been divorced have watched as I did with horrified and disbelieving fascination the transformation of a partner they have loved and thought they knew into someone whose behavior now seems totally foreign, whose view of shared events is so skewed from their own that it is almost impossible to reconcile the two.

Privately held, these misperceptions might be painful enough as evidence that the intimate knowledge that marriage partners thought they had of their spouse's thoughts was both fleeting and false. But when such views are presented in the context of the divorce proceedings as fact, all sorts of emotions are stirred up. This issue commonly causes a huge amount of hurt and anger in the lives of those who find themselves divorced or divorcing.

During the last six or seven years of our marriage, Claire often portrayed me as a religious fanatic—a tyrant even. I believed this so false and so unfair that I felt tremendous anger. This image of me was exactly the opposite of how I viewed myself, and it pushed every emotional hot button I had.

In the past, I had often responded to such situations by giving aggressive verbal vent to my emotions. Now, I sensed retaliating was not the right thing to do, but I had no idea how to avoid doing so. I felt impressed that God didn't want me to defend myself, that I should leave the vindication of my character to Him. Wanting to walk with God, I put real effort into self-control. But doing so left me with a surplus of residual anger that I simply stuffed down with my own human willpower. I didn't understand that such a course is not only unsustainable in human strength but also actually harmful, because it made me bitter and resentful, and sooner or later I'd just give way to another verbal tirade.

Sound familiar? If venting our feelings isn't God's plan for us, and stuffing anger down isn't either, what should we do? Let's explore a better way to deal with anger.

All of us realize the destructive potential of uncontrolled anger. We've heard stories of one party or the other losing all control and behaving violently. While people can express anger in a number of ways, uncontrolled anger always seems somehow to match up with the letter "D" for danger, both for those who are out of control and for those around them. Angry people frequently hurt those they claim to love. An old oriental proverb says, "Anger is an evil wind that blows out the lamp of the mind." And Wayne W. Dyer, in his book *Your Erroneous Zone,* says, "Anger is an erroneous zone, a kind of psychological influenza that incapacitates you just as a physical disease would. . . . Anger is a choice, as well as a habit. It is a learned reaction to frustration, in which you behave in ways that you would rather not. In fact, severe anger is a form of insanity."

Be angry, but don't sin

God is so concerned about human anger that the Bible mentions it 276 times. Paul wrote, " 'In your anger do not sin' " (Ephesians 4:26).

This alone is an astonishing statement, for it tells us that while anger will arise in our lives, we can experience it without sinning. Clearly, God has a different experience of anger in mind than what we generally have gone through. A Bible paraphrase puts it this way: "If you get upset, don't focus on your feelings until they become hateful and degenerate into sin. Be angry with sin, but don't sin by becoming angry with the sinner."

When I saw this, I said, "Lord, I've been married to that woman for more than thirty years. She knows all my hot buttons, and she's pushing them. I feel out of control and ready to lose it without even a conscious thought. I don't know if I can control it, Lord. Take, for example, the other day, when she claimed to have helped me build our real estate investments over nearly a twenty-year period. It's true that she was a great help in the beginning, but after the first three years, she wouldn't even answer the phone or involve herself if the call was related to real estate. It just burns me up!"

"Dick, this isn't the first situation with your wife in which you became angry and raised your voice, is it?"

"Well, no, Lord, it isn't. But what has that got to do with—"

"Do you ever remember arguing with a raised voice when the phone's ring interrupted your argument?"

I thought about it but didn't answer.

"Dick, how did you answer the phone? In an angry tone? With a raised voice?"

"Well . . . no."

"That's right. You had an instant transformation to being cheerful and pleasant. What do you suppose such actions said to Claire about how much you valued her as opposed to the stranger who might be calling? You *can* control your anger. That's not the question, is it? No, it's whether you want to."

"I guess I do, Lord. But what do I do in this heart-breaking situation?"

There was no immediate answer, but the next day I read in my Bible calendar: "The Lord is close to the broken-hearted and saves those who are crushed in spirit." This started me studying to find out how to overcome my anger. If God was going to save me, He must have a plan for overcoming in His strength rather than through my old "grit your teeth" method.

In Romans 12:2, I found that I was to be transformed by the renewing of my mind. It dawned on me that God wanted to teach me to see the circumstances triggering my anger with a new attitude. I saw that this was an absolute necessity because our thoughts form our behavior. In my old way of living, even though I claimed to be a Christian, I often saw only the faults of the other person and felt justified in my response. However, when I consent to have God renew my mind, I can see and respond from His perspective. Then I can see clearly my ugly behavior, my destructive and demeaning words, and my self-centered attitude for what they really are, and I wish to have nothing more to do with them.

The Bible says, "You were taught, with regard to your former way of life, to put off your old self, which is being corrupted by its deceitful desires; to be made new in the attitude of your minds; and to put on the new self, created to be like God in true righteousness and holiness" (Ephesians 4:22–24). In other words, when we face whatever it is that angers us, God is willing to redirect our minds.

This passage speaks of "deceitful desires," which truly fits anger. We think that in expressing it we are going to gain some great good and prove a point or defend ourselves, but we believe a lie. Expressed anger that is uncontrolled leaves in its wake nothing but lives robbed of peace and a huge gulf of separation between the parties. The only message communicated is the anger expressed in the explosion.

In place of this kind of anger, we can have a controlled righteous anger at the sin that lies behind frustrating situations. It's all right to hate the situation and to be angry at the unfair things others do, but hating the person cuts off all communication that could resolve the conflict. Parents cannot but feel anger over divorce as their innocent children suffer. This is normal, and when sublimated into productive, helpful actions and words, this type of righteous anger can be a strong force for good. God tells us, "Do not let any unwholesome talk come out of your mouths, but only what is helpful for building others up according to their needs" (Ephesians 4:29). Viewed objectively, many of the things we argue about are minor issues. When we continually major in the minors, soon everything becomes a major issue even though it doesn't need to be.

Dead to destructive anger

Paul has told us, "We know that our old self was crucified with him so that the body of sin might be done away with, that we should no longer be slaves to sin" (Romans 6:6). If we allow our corrupt self-will to die so God's will can dominate, then our old responses of anger will become powerless to manipulate us. This is truly wonderful news—but to make sure we don't miss the point, the Bible continues: ". . . because anyone who has died has been freed from sin [those old destructive behaviors]" (verse 7).

I pictured my father. He had died and been set free from the terrible burden of pain that his flesh caused him, and here was God's Word saying that God desires the same freedom for me. I could be free from the destructive uncontrolled anger that tried to rule my flesh and make my life—and Claire's—miserable. It seemed amazing that I had never seen this practical truth in these familiar texts. The message was unmistakable, for the passage concludes: "Therefore do not let sin reign in your mortal body so that you obey its evil desires" (verse 12).

Nothing could have been clearer. I had a choice. Through God's presence in us, He has created a way to prevent anger from ruining our peace and our lives. He doesn't remove from our experience the things that stir up angry feelings. Instead, He has provided us with a mechanism to deal with our feelings rather than just to stuff them down or to let them explode. At last, I was learning that "a fool gives full vent to his anger, but a wise man keeps himself under control" (Proverbs 29:11) and that "an angry . . . hot-tempered one commits many sins" (Proverbs 29:22).

Later, as I completed my advanced degrees in Christian psychology and counseling, I learned that secular research has demonstrated an interesting fact about expressed anger. We may feel we need to get what angers us off our chest or even to get revenge, and some excuse their outbursts by saying, "Well, at least I'm not keeping it all bottled up inside." However, not only is doing so not godly, but it brings the opposite of the desired relief from such feelings! Modern studies are now confirming that just as suppressing anger is destructive, so is expressing it. To make matters worse, those who vent their anger actually create more angry feelings in themselves.

It was hard for me to give up defending myself and allow what I felt was terrible misrepresentation to go on with only controlled and quiet responses. I found it difficult to deny my desire to vent my feelings. Many times self clamored to be allowed to justify itself and stay angry. But I was slowly learning—however imperfectly—to die to self and to trust God's presence reigning within me. Where anger was justified, I was learning to respond in constructive ways. I was also learning that injustice, rejection, frustration, and fear always triggered my anger, but that when I let Christ's strength dominate in me, I was no longer so vulnerable to such triggers. Instead, I was able to begin communicating my hurts rather than my anger. If you could look at a video of my life back then, you would see a man walking a tightrope and falling often but getting back on and continuing the course God had set for him. Gradually, it did become easier, although the habits of a lifetime aren't easy to overcome.

You'll likely face a similar struggle if you decide you don't want to give rein to anger anymore. God will be with you. It may seem that you're putting forth your best, heaven-led efforts at civility and kindness only to see them thrown back at you in contempt by a partner who doesn't understand why you are suddenly changing—who thinks you are just being deceptive or trying to manipulate people. But rest assured that others, both in this world and in the heavenly places, also see your struggles. They note with joy and gladness the progress you make, no matter how small the steps.

At the time of my divorce, I was blessed in having older children. One of my sons wrote me a letter that cheered my spirits. I share it so that others may also be encouraged.

Dear Dad,

If I could share your pain and burden, I would. It hurts me to see you and Mom separate, especially when I saw pain in your eyes. I frequently ask God why such tragedy happened to you and Mom. I still don't know why, but one thing I know for sure: during your trial and tribulation, God's even closer to you.

Every night I pray for you to be strong and I ask God to comfort you during your difficult moments. Dad, I pray that in time God will heal your pain. At this point in your life, you are going through the same type of turmoil as Job went through, but in the end, you will receive abundant blessing. Whatever happens, Dad, you're always in my heart and soul. Please take care of yourself.

Others will see your trials too, whether or not they express it quite like my son did. His words, as well as those of my other children, encouraged me. But even more than kind words, it was God's presence and His work of changing me that was most encouraging. I was more at peace with God and my fellow human beings. Even Claire, who suffered the most from my anger, seemed relieved. I know now that the true antidote for self-centered anger is faith in the continual presence of God's transforming peace, which gives us the confidence to be vulnerable and the ability to package our responses in a calm, loving way. It teaches us to express hurts and feelings rather than anger. Through God's power, I had begun to break the cycle of failure that led to my giving way to anger, and you can too.

We may think ourselves justified in becoming angry and venting—and perhaps sometimes we may be. In the end, however, we and the people in our lives benefit more from the high and noble pathway to which God is calling us. James concludes the matter this way: "My dear brothers, take note of this: Everyone should be quick to listen, slow to speak and slow to become angry, for man's anger does not bring about the righteous life that God desires" (James 1:19, 20). I pray that God's desire that you be freed from destructive anger may become a living reality in your experience.

CHAPTER 5

The Excruciating Pain of the Darkness Within

The divorce proceedings dragged on. For the most part, Claire and I were still living together. She knew separation was coming and was making final plans to leave, but I was still hoping against hope that things might work out. There were moments when we seemed like an intact couple doing ordinary things—having breakfast together, discussing the news. However, though I hated to admit it, it was becoming clear even to me that the marriage was finished. Strangely, the bonds of allegiance and commitment I felt to our marriage wouldn't die. My mind now understood the inevitable, but my heart didn't seem to get the message. It constantly hoped for a miracle and continually hurt when one didn't come. I wrote in my journal: "What a fool I am—I never stop hoping. . . . I can only thank You, Lord, that I don't hate her, but it is still so painful."

Sometimes when Claire had left for work, particularly if she'd been exceptionally "distant," the full weight of this terrible pain washed over me. The loss of our marriage threatened to crush me. Even worse, I grieved for the heartache that the destruction of our marriage was causing our precious family. All I could sense was a terrible darkness swirling around me. Even on sunny days, all I could see was gloom! I cried and cried until I was exhausted. Then I dried my tears. What was the use? "Lord, this two-year nightmare seems never ending. If it weren't for my children, I'd beg for death right away. Everything that makes life worth living is gone. I have nothing left—nothing at all." Hurting had almost become a way of life for me, and depression hounded my every move. It was my new dance partner in everything I did.

My children's pain

I hated to see my children suffer as the holidays came and went. At times, their pain seemed even more acute than my own. Poor Tina cried for two hours before we went to my brother's house on Thanksgiving. She'd had to leave her first family when she was only eleven, and now she was losing her new family too.

"It's just not fair, Lord!" I cried out. "All my children hurt; all of them are in tears. The pain is the same on all sides. Some Thanksgiving! Every one of us loses." I tried to understand, but understanding wouldn't come. The weight of it all was too much, so I left the Thanksgiving festivities early.

By the time I got home, I felt like a dead man nearly suffocating in grief and utterly alone. I was literally short of breath. *I wonder if I'm actually dying. Nobody knows that I'm dying all alone,* I thought. "Lord," I prayed, "I need to open my Bible, but my mind goes blank. I need to pray, but my mind wanders and my prayers trail off into nothingness. Is this all I have to look forward to for the rest of my life? Is there to be nothing but gloom and heartache, pain and suffering?" I looked down at my hand and envisioned an empty space where my wedding ring now was. It seemed so odd and unnatural. Perhaps it was a fitting metaphor for what had become of all my hopes and dreams. I felt like Abraham Lincoln, who said, "I am the most miserable man living. If what I feel were equally distributed to the whole human family, there would not be a cheerful face on earth."

When my emotions settled down somewhat, I searched the Bible for comfort. There I read that I wasn't the only one who's ever had to deal with depression. Job said, " 'Why did I not perish at birth . . . ? For now I would be lying down in peace; I would be asleep and at rest. . . . My groans pour out like water. What I feared has come upon me; . . . I have no peace, no quietness; I have no rest, but only turmoil' " (Job 3:11–26).

However, there's another side to this question of trials and adversity. Shakespeare once wrote, "Sweet are the uses of adversity." To most of us, that doesn't make sense. Yet, as hard as it was for me to believe, depression can be an important steppingstone that enables us to come closer to God. Depression can tear down the arrogance and self-confidence that tend to isolate us from Him. So, when rightly understood, such terrible trials—and they are terrible—can act a part in our learning process.

God doesn't will that we be depressed. But when we are depressed, He desires that we learn from the experience. Paul talked of this very process: "We do not want you to be uninformed, brothers, about the hardships we suffered in the province of Asia. We were under great pressure, . . . so that we despaired even of life. [I could relate to that.] Indeed, in our hearts we felt the sentence of death. But this happened that we might not rely on ourselves, but on God, who raises the dead. . . . and he will deliver us" (2 Corinthians 1:8–10).

The apostle Paul's words riveted my attention: "This happened that we might not rely on ourselves." God was teaching me not only to rely totally on Him in my despair and hopelessness but also that He was going to deliver me from my anguish and give me a new life. For the first time, I cried tears of hope.

Depression is a normal reaction to a tragic loss. Does this mean that those who are going through or have come through a divorce are without God? Is that why they tend to become depressed? Absolutely not! When we suffer a loss, we grieve, and the stage of depression is often the longest one of this process. However, by our choices we can indulge our feelings of self-pity and prolong what should be just a *chapter* of our life into a *continuing* experience. In his book *Spirit-Controlled*

Temperament, Dr. Tim LaHaye eloquently voices this concern about-non-physically induced depression. He states: "A person becomes depressed after a period of indulging in one of the most subtle sins of all—self-pity."

You can see the danger right away. The self-pitying thoughts affect our very hearts and souls and turn our thoughts not heavenward but inward, toward what the self wants and desires. The problem is that all too often in the situation of divorce, what self wants is counterproductive and not in line with God's leading. How much better it would be to adopt the attitude Jesus expressed when He said, "Not My will but Thine be done." Choosing this attitude would fortify us for the self-denial required to exercise patience, kindness, and gentleness when dealing with our former spouse. It would enable us to deal with the financial, property, and visitation issues in a more unemotional, constructive, and equitable manner. This better attitude means choosing to do God's will no matter how despicably, how unfairly, or how meanly we feel we've been treated. That's what Jesus meant when He told us to follow Him by denying self and taking up our cross (see Luke 9:23). In this case, the cross we have to take up may be a painful divorce.

What does this mean? Denying self allows Christ to live in us. The apostle Paul explained it this way: "I have been crucified with Christ. I no longer live but Christ lives in me" (Galatians 2:20). The cross we have to take up is learning to trust ourselves and our circumstances into His perfect care—no matter what the cost. "It is God who works in you to will and to act according to His good purposes" (Philippians 2:13).

When it isn't God's plan

"But, Richard," I can hear you say, "you told me God didn't design that I get divorced, so how can I do His will for me when I'm going through something He never wanted for me?"

57

This is a fair question. The answer is found in Ephesians 1:11, which tells us that God "works out everything in conformity with the purpose of his will." In other words, God didn't want you to suffer what you're going through. He didn't cause your situation. Divorce almost always results from self-centered human choices. Yet God allows us the freedom to choose and to act as we desire. He, in turn, is a master planner and restorer. He takes the tragedies of our lives and transforms them so that they can serve His purpose for us. If we could see the end from the beginning, we'd realize that His plans are always the best for our happiness. He tells us, " 'I know the plans I have for you, . . . plans to prosper you and not to harm you, plans to give you hope and a future. Then you will call upon me and come and pray to me, and I will listen to you' " (Jeremiah 29:11, 12).

If you think you are the exception to this text, as I did, I'd like to encourage you otherwise. In those terrible, dark hours, I couldn't see any way God's plans could possibly give me hope and a future. But our objections have a way of shrinking into insignificance when faced with the test of time, while God's promises, without exception, always prove true. When I look back now after the passage of just a few years, I'm awed at what God has done in my life. If we could talk face to face with Jesus in our times of heartache, I'm sure He would respond to us as He did to Peter: " 'You do not realize now what I am doing, but later you will understand' " (John 13:7).

The next question that arose in my mind went something like this: "OK, Lord, I don't understand why this has happened to me. I realize that someday I will understand, but that doesn't make it any easier for me to go through it right now! I know I want to die to self. That is my desire and my goal. However, while my future seems dark and foreboding, I'm not supposed to indulge in self-pity. But I have to do something! Exactly what am I supposed to do in my situation?"

"Richard," came the reply, "I never ask anything of you without providing the power for you to accomplish it. But even more to the point, Richard, I ask you to allow Me to live in you so you may die to self and experience true happiness. Have you ever noticed that you can never fully satisfy your self-will, your desires, and your wishes? If you want a new shirt and you finally get it, you often find either that you don't like it as much as you thought you would or that you like it and want still more clothes. The same is true in every area of your being. I ask you to die to self so that you can be free from serving a power that is a tyrant in its demands. Whatever I ask of you, I ask to prevent self from ruling in your life.

"I know your ex doesn't presently follow the same program, and, at least in your eyes, she is making you miserable. But if you will trust Me and agree to die to self, you'll find that you can choose not to respond negatively to her but with gentleness and self-controll. In fact, you'll find that it isn't what others may try to do to you that makes you miserable. Rather, it's your indulgence of self-pity and the resulting depression that has that effect. You're going to have to be willing to trust Me. Trust that I know best and that I'll get you through this while transforming you into a reflection of My character."

"That's encouraging, Lord, but what part do I play?"

"Richard, if you'll read Philippians 2:14, I think you'll understand. It says, 'Do everything without complaining or arguing.' Why? Because complaining is a form of rebellion against the things I've allowed. All you do in your moaning and groaning and complaining is to hinder what I'd like to do in you. In doing so, you prolong your time of sorrow and deepen your suffering. ' "Forget the former things; do not dwell on the past. See, I am doing a new thing!" ' (Isaiah 43:18, 19)."

I must confess that the idea that by complaining about my current situation I was delaying my return to happiness really struck home. I was so unhappy that I didn't want to stay as I was for a moment longer. I started making up little reminders for myself that said "No MGC" (moaning, groaning, and complaining). I posted these reminders everywhere, from the bathroom mirror to my wallet and calendar.

Although I was still tempted to solicit the pity of others, giving up complaining out loud was the easiest part of this change. I found it a lot harder to stop complaining inwardly and indulging in my own private pity party. However, with my constant reminders and my earnest desire to follow God and have His peace, it got easier. With God's presence in my life, I at last was able to put moaning, groaning, and complaining behind me.

Then I found to my dismay that "the past" was exactly where my thoughts tended to dwell! This was understandable. It was in the past that I had been "happy" and, more recently, that's when I'd been hurt. The future seemed so unreal to me, and the present seemed to be such a time of endless pain that I wanted to retreat into the fantasy of my "happy" past. The Lord finally got through to me that driving a car while concentrating upon the rearview mirror is not only hard, it's downright dangerous! The lesson was clear, so I read Philippians 3:12, 13 over and over again: "Press on to take hold of that for which Christ Jesus took hold of me. . . . Forgetting what is behind and straining toward what is ahead."

I'm not saying that it's easy to die to self and receive a new heart from God. To be honest, it's the hardest thing I've ever chosen to allow God to do in me. But it's also the only way I've ever found true peace— and I found it even amid the depressing circumstances of a divorce. God knew us before we were ever formed. He knew what would happen to us, and nothing has surprised Him nor have His plans for us as His children been altered. He loves you regardless of your marital status, and He longs to lead you out of your pit of depression and to fill your life with His love, joy, and peace.

Psalm 40:1–3 says, "He turned to me and heard my cry. He lifted me out of the slimy pit, out of the mud and mire; he set my feet on the rock and gave me a firm place to stand. He put a new song in my mouth, a hymn of praise to our God." I found this to be true, and it is my heartfelt wish that you'll permit God to begin the same mighty work in your life. All that is required is your willingness to trust Him.

CHAPTER 6

Learning to Follow God in Loneliness

After years of false hopes, the end was in sight for my marriage. We sold the house, and I moved to Florida to be near my son, hoping that distance and time would help me heal.

Not too long after moving, I wrote, "I've found that distance has not solved anything for me. I may have moved to Florida, but the pain of loneliness has once again ambushed me with a new, unexpected vengeance. I realize that the past few weeks have been a turning point from the past and the beginning point of looking to the future. The question is: What do I do with the present? How do I cope with this never-ending loneliness that is becoming my new existence? Where do I find the strength to get through this seemingly endless and heartbreaking period in my life?"

Mother Teresa said, "Loneliness and the feeling of being unwanted is the most terrible poverty." How does one willingly embrace that which one fears? I didn't know how to submit to God in this area. Loneliness attacked me without mercy, imprisoning and crushing me into nothingness. Only those who have entered into this desperate struggle fully understand that loneliness is a tenacious foe that clings to one like the darkness does to night. It is capable of placing one in solitary confinement even while among other people. It kept me awake at night as the tape of my past played over and over with no off button. I couldn't sleep and couldn't eat, and when I did succumb to sleep out of total exhaustion, I would awake in the middle of the night in tears. Repeatedly, I tried to understand what had gone wrong after so many years of marriage—where I had failed and what I could have done differently. But no matter how brilliant my analysis, it was too late. I began to desire death as a blessed relief from my pain, and I seemed to be drifting further from God and not closer.

I related so deeply to what David wrote; he and I would have been good friends. "Turn to me and be gracious to me, for I am lonely and afflicted. The troubles of my heart have multiplied; free me from my anguish" (Psalm 25:16, 17). "Why haven't you come to save me? Why are you so far away? Haven't you heard my groaning? O my God! I cry out by day, but you don't answer. I cry out at night but get no response. . . . My strength and courage are gone. They have drained from my body like water from a broken jar. . . . I feel as if you've left me lying in the dust to die" (Psalm 22:1, 2, 14, 15, *Clear Word*).

My whole focus shifted toward the pain and loneliness I was suffering. My thoughts turned so far inward that prayer became increasingly difficult, and at times, I couldn't even read the Bible. I was sinking in the quicksand of depression, and it seemed I could do nothing to stop myself.

I remained in this despairing state for many weeks while I questioned God's love for me. Then it seemed as if God opened a little window, and I caught a vision of Christ in the Garden that fateful night, struggling to decide whether He was willing to embrace what was coming. I could picture Him being tortured to death and willingly embracing it all just so He could reach down and save people like me!

Embrace loneliness?

After this experience, I never questioned God's love for me, but I still struggled with the question of how I could willingly embrace my loneliness. I'd like to tell you that I had a sudden transformation of attitude and thoughts, but we humans tend to be too set in our ways for such things to happen. Instead, the Lord repeated again and again the lessons He was trying to teach me, until at last they began to sink into my thick skull and some new revelations dawned. God knows that if He were to solve every issue and problem for us instantly, we'd be deprived of valuable lessons.

I came to realize that God knows the full course of our lives and that my divorce didn't take Him by surprise. He also worked to get me to see that my self-centered responses were making things worse for me, not better. I'd been responding as if I had to handle my situation in my own strength and wisdom. Unfortunately, the really valuable lessons seem to come in our times of suffering. But for me to gain from my experience—even this experience of loneliness that I loathed—I had to enter it as a willing participant.

The spiritual writer and speaker Joni Eareckson Tada once said, "We are not responsible for circumstances, but we are responsible for our responses." This was the key I had been missing. God knew what was going to happen to me, and He had a plan to get me through it. " 'I am the Lord your God, who teaches you what is best for you, who directs you in the way you should go' " (Isaiah 48:17). "Endure hardship as discipline. . . . No discipline seems pleasant at the time, but painful. Later on, however, it produces a harvest of righteousness and peace for those who have been trained by it" (Hebrews 12:7, 11).

Having reached the end of my rope and finding that nothing I did was improving my situation, at long last I consented to accept my lot in life. I consented to embrace my suffering as something that God was allowing into my life, something that somehow He would work for my own good, although that concept was purely intellectual at this early stage. All my emotions could see were years of solitary misery stretching out before me. But when I accepted loneliness as God's choice for me, much of its force was blunted. I learned to accept the pain loneliness caused, trusting that God was going to use my circumstances to do a mighty work in my life and make me a blessing to others. I realized that no matter what mistakes I had made, no matter how fate or circumstances had seemed to conspire against me, God was in charge of my life. As the Bible says, "God . . . works in you to will and to act according to his good purpose" (Philippians 2:13).

The words in the next verse shocked me: "Do everything without complaining or arguing." I thought of all the weeks I had wallowed about miserably, and I realized that not one of my sleepless nights had done me one bit of good. They had, in fact, harmed me terribly. You see, as human souls, we are little more than our thoughts and feelings. When I allowed my thoughts to dwell upon my unhappy circumstances, they affected my attitude—not only my attitude about life in general, but even about God. After all, when I'm dwelling on myself and fretting about my problems, I'm certainly not acting as if I trust God to work out all things for the good.

My negative thoughts bore fruit in negative feelings that created negative actions and reactions, which, in turn, fed even more thoughts that were negative. I was in a never-ending cycle designed by the enemy of my soul to make my problems become increasingly bigger and more unmanageable. This in turn made me feel entirely hopeless and my future even darker.

God's simple promise stands in contrast to this desperate cycle: " 'My grace is sufficient for you, for my power is made perfect in [your] weakness' " (2 Corinthians 12:9). There were many times when I thought that the depth of my loneliness was going to test this promise of sustaining power beyond its ability to bear. But I can testify that the deeper my despair became, the more I experienced the evidence of Christ's strength in me—as long as I was willing to surrender self so He could continue to live in me. And whenever I started up my old familiar pity party, feeling lonely and unfairly oppressed, the Lord was always there, reminding me to " 'Forget the former things; do not dwell on the past. See, I am doing a new thing [in you]!' " (Isaiah 43:18, 19). God kept telling me, "I am trying to transform you into a new person, and when you dwell on yourself and your past, you hinder My transforming work."

I discovered that I could deal with the painful memories that haunted me during my sleepless nights not by trying to shut them out but by dwelling on God and His presence. When we continually deal with our pain, troubles, and failures in the strength of God's loving presence, they lose their power over us. God continually longs to embrace us with the security and peace of His love. Listen to Him speak: " 'I have loved you with an everlasting love; I have drawn you with loving-kindness' " (Jeremiah 31:3). Whenever I lost my focus on this thought, I moved away from God back into my old self-destructive ways. You see, loneliness is a vacuum that needs to be filled. If we don't fill it with God, we'll fit it with just about anything else—alcohol, drugs, illicit relationships, and especially depression.

We have a tendency to think that we're the only ones who have ever suffered so terrible a loss, and we can find any number of reasons why our situation is worse than everybody else's. But God says that nothing happens to us except that which is common to our fellow men and women (see 1 Corinthians 10:13). Some experts who have studied loneliness believe that at any given time, as many as 25 percent of the adult population is lonely. For some, this fact can be a depressing thought because it takes away our rationale for playing the martyr and having a pity party about our lot in life. Yet understanding this fact can be one of the first steps to surviving loneliness. Others have survived what you are going through, and you can too.

The choice I faced

When in my loneliness things seemed as dark as they could become, I realized I faced a choice. I could accept my situation as something God had allowed and trust that He knew more than I did about the effect this would have on my future happiness. Or I could reject the idea that the misery I was going through could have a positive effect upon me and simply struggle on until things somehow improved . . . maybe. It was a hard battle fought in my mind, for as much as I strove to see things objectively, I could see no possibility of any positive outcome in my loneliness. It wasn't until I learned to turn those dreadful hours of loneliness into majestic moments of aloneness with God that I began to understand that my time of suffering was the only time I would be willing to learn to draw closer to Him. I decided that if I was going to suffer, I at least wanted my suffering to serve a constructive purpose. So, eventually, I decided to trust God and believe that what had happened to me would have a net positive effect upon my life. I must admit my belief wavered sometimes, but when confronted with the alternative, with increasing frequency I chose to yield to what God was trying to do in my life.

I soon found that accepting God's gift of faith not only enabled me to trust Him but it also gave me strength and courage to exchange my will for His. I didn't fully understand it at the time, but having faith to trust in God's knowledge and power over and above my own and yielding to what He was doing in my life was my first major step into the real Christian life. For the first time in my life, I trusted God enough to be truly willing to surrender all my hopes, desires, and dreams. As hard as it was for me to lay down my own wishes for my life, I found in the very act of surrender an inner peace and even joy with God I hadn't known before. The burden of running my own life lifted from me as I placed it in God's hands, and for the first time in years, the stress I had been living under began to ease.

This surrender marked the beginning of significant changes in my attitude, behavior, and outlook. I began to realize that to hold on to that faith, I must be willing to deny self—that is, to die to my self-centered choices moment by moment throughout the day. As this happened and I allowed God to live in me, my faith grew.

Faith in God is a fragile plant, and the two greatest enemies to maintaining that faith live within the self. The first is fear—fear of trusting the difficult circumstances of our life to God. The second is pride, which is far more subtle than most of us realize. And anger, impatience, unforgiveness, loneliness, and depression are all inseparably linked with pride.

When I was all alone with God in Florida, He began showing me things in myself that I didn't even know were there—distasteful things that I wanted to leave untouched and hidden away. However, gradually, God helped me understand that while evading problems and character faults appeals to our human nature, doing so leaves us totally in their power. I learned that I would find freedom if I would allow Jesus to carry me through the painful process of removing my faults. With this understanding, I began to allow Him to teach me.

The very first thing God led me to was the admonition found in Luke 6:27, 28: " 'Do good to those who hate you, bless those who curse you, pray for those who mistreat you.' "

"But, Lord," I complained, "I have a right to be upset and angry. It is my right to want to get even with Claire for all the loneliness and pain I'm suffering. Be nice? I can never be nice or forgive her for what she has done."

"Richard, remember that just a few months ago you were willing to do almost anything to keep her?"

I hesitated to respond though I knew the answer. At last, I said, "That was before she divorced me!"

"So you were willing to love her if you could get what you wanted?"

I didn't like the trend of this conversation. I much preferred conversing with those who would agree that Claire had done me wrong.

The discomforting counsel continued: " 'Do not repay anyone evil for evil. . . . Do not take revenge. . . . Do not be overcome by evil, but overcome evil with good' " (Romans 12:17, 19, 21).

"Even if I treated her nicely, she wouldn't appreciate it."

"My Word says, 'They claim to know God, but by their actions they deny him' (Titus 1:16). The 'reasons' you've presented are just excuses to avoid doing that which crosses your will. Your rationalizations for avoiding the path of duty are motivated by your pride and your anger. Look at what you're really saying. You're angry because she divorced you—she hurt your pride. Before the divorce, you wanted her back in the worst way. But now, because she crossed your will and hurt your pride, you won't consider forgiving her and treating her as well as or better than when you were trying to win back her affections. You know she suffers as badly as you do, yet you believe that even if you were to treat her well, she would just be hurtful.

"Richard, I want to tell you the secret of loving. To love other people, you must open yourself up to being hurt by them. This is how I love you. No matter how many times you reject Me, I return again and again to try to win your heart. If you respond, I treat you as if you had never rejected Me. Those who truly love never look to the response of the other person to decide if loving was the right thing to do. No, they love even when they know right up front that all they stand to gain is hurt, rejection, and abuse."

God left me to think it through. This was heavy stuff, but eventually I realized He was right. I did fear rejection and more hurt, and I didn't want to open myself up to more pain. Yet that was what God was asking me to do—to open myself to that possibility.

The greatest battle ever fought

About this time in my experience, I read the following passage, which made things clearer to me: "The warfare against self is the greatest battle that was ever fought. The yielding of self, surrendering all to the will of God, requires a struggle; but the soul must submit to God before it can be renewed in holiness."[1]

I wanted this renewal, yet I loathed the surrender that it called for. Still, I began to move toward what God was asking of me. As I did, I would begin in His strength but then soon find myself reverting to my old ways and making a mess of things. I was so ashamed that I thought I couldn't face God after falling flat on my face again and again. But you know, He never once met me with condemnation. He was always there to pick me up, to comfort and lead me in better ways and encourage me that in His strength I could do better than my best. After each time that I failed, I found that I again moved closer to His desires for me. God was teaching me even in my failures that "he saved us, not because of righteous things we had done, but because of his mercy" (Titus 3:5).

Through my own hard and exceedingly lonely experience, I have come to understand that God intends to strengthen us and bring us through the loneliness that encompasses our life. Never forget that God has good plans for us. Remember the text we looked at in the last chapter: " 'For I know the plans I have for you,' declares the Lord, 'plans to prosper you and not to harm you, plans to give you hope and a future' " (Jeremiah 29:11). It is Satan, never God, who is seeking our destruction, and he designs that we shall never be free from the misery that loneliness causes the vast majority of those who are divorced. But there is a way to survive our loneliness and turn what at first we considered a curse into a long-term benefit.

Satan's aim is to destroy hope for the future by bringing to our minds all our faults, real or imagined. He wants to discourage us from seeking God. However, no matter what we've done, no matter what our life's circumstances, God views us in the light of our potential in Him. A master carpenter looking at an old and neglected house notices the defects, but they fade from significance in comparison to the latent potential that only he can see in the ruined structure. In exactly the same way, God wants to restore us in His image. He doesn't care how many defects we have. He doesn't look upon our ruined marriage and hold our past against us. He focuses only upon what we may become under His skillful hand.

What do these hardships train us to do? It is far more than to surrender to God's will. Our loneliness is the perfect training ground on which we can learn to develop a deeply personal relationship with a deeply personal God. Life as most of us have led it is too full of busyness and distractions to allow us the time we need to seek God and know Him in anything more than a superficial manner. Many of these distractions are swept away in the wake of our failed marriage, and if we are willing, God holds out before us the opportunity to enter into an intimate relationship with Him that in some ways can be deeper than any we have ever had even with our former spouse. God knows all about us—more than any human being does. He even knows every secret thought that we've hidden from everyone else. Yet He still loves us and desires our companionship.

So, one of the greatest benefits of loneliness is freedom from many of the things that once distracted us from God. Another is the greater realization of our acute need for His presence in us than we've ever had before. This time of our lives is pregnant with the opportunity to embrace God and to begin allowing Him to alter the present and the future for the better.

We still have more to learn about God, but at this point I believe God would have us understand the distractions that may lie ahead, so in the next chapter we'll look at one of the biggest—relationships!

---

1. Ellen G. White, *Steps to Christ* (Nampa, Idaho: Pacific Press®, n.d.), 43.

Part II:
What I Learned About Divorce

CHAPTER 7

The Right Relationship

"So, Richard, how long do we have to wait to begin a new relationship?"

The sudden silence in the divorce recovery seminar told me Danny had hit on a hot-button issue. While not the topic for the evening, I had to address the group's concern.

"Well, Danny," I replied, "the quick answer is that you're ready for a new relationship when you no longer need one."

Every face showed disappointment, so I continued. "I wish I could provide you a specific formula that would work for every situation. Many Christian counselors try to do just that. The rule of thumb they go by is that you need one year of recovery for every four years of marriage."

Those who had previously looked disappointed now looked appalled as they worked the numbers in their heads. No one had expected such a lengthy time between relationships. I let the numbers sink in for a moment before I disagreed with my fellow counselors.

"Now let me explain why the conventional wisdom doesn't always work," I said. "Our goal before remarriage or anything that might lead to it is not the passage of a certain amount of time but the attainment of a certain new relationship with God. This and this alone is what qualifies you for a new relationship, and this alone will give meaning and value to all you've been through and all you're going to go through. Before you consider developing a new relationship, it is absolutely imperative that you become a secure person in Christ. Allowing Him to fill your emotional, psychological, and spiritual needs will set you free from desperately needing someone else to fill them. This is what I meant when I said you must come to the place of not needing a relationship in order to be ready for one. Obtaining this experience is no easy task because, as you've already found out, it crosses our own will continuously. And it takes not only commitment but also time for God's work to become firmly rooted in us.

"That's why the formula I shared doesn't always work for everyone. If you've lost a twenty-year marriage, the conventional wisdom says you need five years to recover. However, if you're in a fulfilling relationship with God in, say, three years, you have no obligation to wait two more years. Likewise, if you lost your marriage after three years, following the standard formula of a nine-month recovery isn't likely to provide you nearly enough time to build a new relationship with God or to allow the submitting of your will to become a habit."

I left my group with much to think about that night. I couldn't help but ponder my own experience and also the experiences of the many people with whom I've been privileged to work. The problem most of us face after the devastating loss of a marriage is that the old ways in which we tried to meet our very legitimate human needs have failed. If we attempt to find another person to meet those needs before we deal with our past, we're almost certain to fall short of our heart's desire for lasting marital happiness.

Undoubtedly, some of you reading this may wonder why I'm even bringing up the subject of relationships when you probably haven't even recovered from your present one. I know I felt that way. One part of me cried out "No way!" to the idea of a new relationship. But I also felt so empty that the other part yearned to love someone. Someone who would love me, and the sooner the better!

I believe the Creator who designed us placed this yearning in our heart. The desire to be validated, to feel loved, and to love again is completely natural. The problem arises because as we try to fill the huge void left by our divorce, we tend to get the cart in front of the horse. Consequently, instead of solving our problems, we complicate them. What I'm going to share is an attempt to point you in the right direction before you enter a new relationship. If you've already begun one, what follows can help you evaluate its status and viability. Search your heart as you consider the following list of prerequisites concerning a new relationship. If you answer No to any of the questions, you aren't ready for one.

- Are you truly in a growing relationship with God?
- Is your divorce legal and final?
- Have you exhausted all reasonable efforts at reconciliation?
- Have you resolved any substance-abuse problems?
- Is your new household reasonably settled?
- Are you financially solvent?
- Is your relationship with God such that He's now a companion able to fill your needs?
- Are your periods of depression and/or loneliness increasingly fewer and farther between?
- Are your thoughts shifting from what happened in the past to your present and your future?
- Have you applied all the concepts contained in this volume— especially forgiveness?

If you can answer all the above with an honest and wholehearted Yes, then you are ready to explore relationships—*under God's control rather than yours.*

A new mind-set about dating

There is an alternative to the typical dating so common in the world and even the church. But it isn't always popular because it requires that before people go searching for Mr. or Ms. Right, they must believe that the Lord knows who their future mate is, where that person is, and when they should meet him or her. Hence, divorcees need not go looking for that someone special but should instead concentrate on developing their bond of love and trust with God. The stronger their bond with Him becomes, the more likely they'll be ready to recognize the marital partner God has been preparing for them. It's when we learn to trust *whom, when,* and *where* completely to God and not ourselves that we will truly have peace and a promising future.

In this new mind-set, preparation for marriage is not so much finding the right person but being the right person in God. Notice God's promise: "Delight yourself in the Lord and he will give you the desires of your heart. Commit your way to the Lord; trust in him and he will do this" (Psalm 37:4, 5). Likewise, Matthew 6:33 promises that if you " 'seek first his kingdom and his righteousness, [then] all these things will be given to you as well.' "

This orientation changes everything about the dating process. Most significantly, it alters the way in which you will evaluate any potential new partner. It's not that basic chemistry, spark, and attraction play no role, for most certainly you should be attracted to the person you marry. However, you are to hold those things in subjection to the primary qualification in any new relationship, which is that your prospective partner must be committed to having his or her self-will under the control of God. If you've progressed through your divorce to the point of considering a new relationship, you should know what it means to die to self over and over again. While terribly difficult and certainly painful at times, it is this death to self-will and submission to Christ that qualifies you for a new relationship. In looking back over your failed marriage, it shouldn't be hard to realize that self-centeredness on both sides was the root of your trouble, and if you want to avoid a repeat of the past, then you're certainly going to want someone who shows the same self-sacrificial experience with God that you've been learning.

I share the following statistics not to make any of you nervous but to encourage you to consider carefully what truly makes a marriage prosper and to choose a marriage partner wisely. Second marriages fail a staggering 74 percent of the time, while third and fourth marriages have failure rates of 83 and 95 percent respectively. Nevertheless, more than 80 percent of divorced individuals will eventually remarry.

Can second and third marriages last? The answer is Yes! Ensuring the lifelong prosperity of marriages is dependent upon two things— trusting God to bring the marriage partners together, and allowing God to keep them together by changing them on the inside. In other words, to have a successful remarriage, you must be God-centered rather than self-centered. When marriages have this focus, the odds of ever repeating the nightmare of divorce are enormously reduced. The book *Family Foundations* by Paul Meier and Richard Meier states, "Only one out of four hundred marriages ends in divorce when the couple read the Bible and pray together."

You see, when I no longer live my self-centered way but trust Christ to live in me, then I have a real, vital connection with God, who plants in me a self-giving love that will prosper my marriage even through difficult times. God assures us, "I will instruct you and teach you in the way you should go; I will counsel you and watch over you. . . . [My] unfailing love surrounds the man who trusts in [Me]" (Psalm 32:8, 10).

How would you like to live with a spouse who has an unshakable love for God that makes that person gentle and kind, willing to deny self and to consider your needs and feelings before his or her own? A spouse who is cheerful, unfailing, and faithful not just in marriage but in all of his or her obligations; who is honest yet thoughtful? Sounds like a mate made in heaven, right? Wrong! It is a mate right here on earth whom God is leading and in whom His Spirit is dwelling. And God is calling us, you and me, to be just such persons. This is what it means to become a new person in Christ and a loving partner for marriage.

The problem with us is that during most of our lives we have probably acted just as we thought, felt, or desired. I've found that even after going to God and sincerely desiring to have Him lead in my life, my inclinations often pulled me back to my old self-centered ways of thinking and behaving. Let me summarize the apostle Paul's experience and solution to this as seen in chapters 7 and 8 of Romans: "I've blown it again and again. What a wretched man I am! Who can rescue me from myself? Ah ha!—yes: Jesus, my Lord. Now, I am not being controlled by my self-centered nature anymore, but by God's Holy Spirit living in me."

So, don't despair if you find it hard to rely upon God continually, for the enemy of our souls wishes to get us focused upon our shortcomings and upon anything else that will separate us from God. Remember, whenever we realize we have slipped back into our old ways, Jesus invites us to deny self, take up our cross, and follow Him (see Mark 8:34). He is a God of love, mercy, and patience, and He offers as many second chances as we need.

We deny our self-will every time we choose to abandon our self-centered ways and trust God to renew us with His amazing grace. This battle with self is the greatest battle we'll ever fight because it's so natural for us to demand what we want when we want it. We see this sinful characteristic in all human beings from the time they are infants. Now, as we are deciding of our own free wills to call upon God to crucify these selfish characteristics for what is perhaps the first time in twenty, thirty, or even forty years, it is no wonder that we struggle against long-standing, habitual behaviors. It's a struggle that no human can wage successfully apart from the power of God. If you decide to engage in this warfare, know with certainty that even with divine power interceding on your behalf, you will have a difficult and at times a painful struggle before you experience the joy of victory.

When we have tasted of this experience, we can better understand why the apostle Paul said, "I have been crucified with Christ and I no longer live, but Christ lives in me" (Galatians 2:20). Paul had come to understand this battle we are now entering. He had learned how to live his life under the control of another—not as a slave who has no control over who ruled him, but as a free moral agent who chose to submit to the love and wisdom of God and reaffirm that choice whenever he felt the inclination to do things his own way.

When Paul said "I am crucified," he meant "I am choosing the pain of putting my desires to death so I may emerge from this torture living a new life filled with Christ's attributes of love, joy, and peace." Paul made this choice because he knew the immense joy and peace that comes from having an all-knowing and loving God guide him through all his situations and circumstances in ways he could never have envisioned. A Christian is very much like a woman in labor who accepts pain that she may bring forth a new life.

If you have walked this road of self-denial, you know what I am speaking about. If not, you are not only missing heaven's richest blessing upon your life but you are also markedly increasing the chances that you will repeat the painful failures of the past—something none of us want.

Finding the right person

You might ask, "But Richard, how do I go about allowing God to lead me to the right person for remarriage? Don't I have to do something? How much responsibility do I have, and how much is God's? If I stay home and never take any action that will bring me in contact with other people, it's unlikely that my potential mate will appear suddenly at my door."

That is entirely correct. We do have a role to play. God expects us to do our part by being willing to meet others and to give others a chance to get to know us, all the while treating each person we meet with respect, dignity, and love as would befit a son or daughter of the King. In God's time, He'll put you in contact with your potential mate. You don't have to become anxious or go searching desperately. Just let all those whom you meet see God's grace growing in you. He'll do the rest. Searching for the right mate is not your responsibility; being God's child is.

I strongly encourage you to get to know a variety of people in a casual group setting. This avoids the exclusivity of a traditional "date" and helps prevent your bonding to someone before you've had opportunity to observe his or her character and spirituality fully. It usually takes a couple of months to do this. Take your time; remember, you are investing for the long term. Anyone can look good for a week or two, but over a longer period, few can keep up a front long enough to prevent you from seeing who they really are.

However, if as a result of your observations and conversations over several months you are impressed that you both relate to each other in a godly way—by which I mean, both of you are respectful and spiritually uplifting to the other—if you are mutually attracted to each other's character and spiritual life, consider beginning an exclusive, but casual relationship and see if it continues to grow. When such a friendship shows potential to be more than casual, be sure to include God in a more positive but gentle way. Include Him not only during your usual courting activities but also by doing such spiritual things together as reading the Bible and good spiritual literature, watching inspirational videos, participating in church activities, going on mission trips, and of course, praying together. Your relationship with a potential mate should encourage within both of you the growth of God's presence. If it doesn't, if you draw each other away from God rather than inclining each other toward Him, then you should seriously consider abandoning the relationship.

If you have covered these early steps and God seems to be blessing your relationship, the question of becoming more serious naturally arises. We'd like to think that having been married and having experienced a long-term relationship is an advantage, but in some ways it can work against us, particularly if we rush through the early days of courtship looking for the deeper intimacy and trust we remember and miss so much from our married life. Unfortunately, it takes time to get to know—I mean really know—another person. Most of my clients find they need seven hundred to eight hundred hours of contact before they can begin to decide about marriage. This takes a year or more. During this time, trying situations will test both of you. How you each manage them will reveal the degree to which self is willing to die and how strongly God's love is present in both of you.

After you've successfully invested some months in casual group dating and a year or more dating exclusively, you need to move your relationship forward toward marriage. The inability to do so constitutes a strong warning that your relationship lacks viability. If God has given you both confidence and the fullness of His peace, you should proceed to engagement. The clients of mine who have the best outcomes seem to opt for an engagement of about six months.

Will these guidelines work? Yes, when people use them under God's influence. But beware of some typical minefields along the way. It is far too easy to fall into minimizing, rationalizing, or rushing the critical first step of beginning to die to self before any courtship begins. God can't perform some magical transformation in our lives to prepare us for a fulfilled life-long marriage when we avoid this first step. Another danger is the failure to wait for the Lord to lead us to a mate. It's hard to wait! I know, for I've stood in your shoes. However, this waiting time can be a most precious time—a time when God does His important work of transforming us to will and act according to His perfect love. Don't waste this opportunity.

Unless the Lord is building your relationship, you can't expect to have a prosperous lifelong marriage. Always remember that a Christian marriage is two sinners—not two saints—coming together, desiring with all their hearts for God to continue His transforming work of crucifying self so that His love lives in them, equipping them for the tough times—which will come.

Dating's impact on your children

If you have children, you need to realize that they will likely find any such new relationship very difficult and confusing. After the breakup of their home, your children will need some years of stability to become secure once more, so you must put off dating for an extended period. Of course, there are other concerns you should keep in mind when you are prayerfully convinced that the time is right to commence dating. Children whose parents have divorced feel that they've already lost one parent, so, as the custodial parent dates, they will very likely feel as if they're losing that parent too. Regardless of how nice the person you're dating is, your children's feelings of abandonment can have some serious psychological and emotional ramifications, so go very slowly here. Give highest priority to the well-being of your children. This is an area fraught with dangers; stepchild relationships are a major cause of subsequent divorces.

Currently, 70 percent of all couples live together before marrying, and the numbers are believed to be higher among the previously divorced. But if your goal is to remarry and then keep that marriage permanent and prospering, I suggest that you shouldn't count on the idea that living together first will help. People who do so are likely to be disappointed. Research has found that those who lived together before marriage experience substantially higher divorce rates than those who didn't.

People who are sincerely seeking to follow God's leading in their life know that living together before marriage is not God's plan for us. In fact, the Bible tells us that He condemns such arrangements. I believe He does this because it is not an effective way for us to move toward a fulfilled and successful marriage, and He desires our long-term happiness.

The very nature of living together before marriage has major inherent weaknesses. One is the lack of a serious covenant with God and one's mate to remain committed even during the difficult times. Another is that the cohabiting couple doesn't enjoy the fullness of God's marital blessings, which would carry them through the rough times and enable the bonds of love between the two of them and between them and God to grow stronger.

Emotions are one of romance's greatest joys and greatest dangers. There is nothing wrong with the wonderful feelings associated with romance—God created them. However, a relationship based solely upon emotions can look very much like the real thing without having any of the underlying strength of a true, God-based relationship. Emotional ties may appear to be as strong as steel, but time has repeatedly demonstrated that relationships based upon feelings cannot long endure the stresses that come to every couple sooner or later. Then the couple finds that in place of the steel they thought they had, their ties shatter like crystal.

The true strength of relationship comes from the presence of God's love in us. He has described that love: "Love is patient, love is kind. It does not envy, it does not boast, it is not proud. It is not rude, it is not self-seeking, it is not easily angered, it keeps no record of wrongs. Love does not delight in evil but rejoices with the truth. It always protects, always trusts, always hopes, always perseveres" (1 Corinthians 13:4–7).

The type of love God gives us is not based upon romantic feelings but rather on self-denying actions. Romantic feelings are a delightful benefit of a self-denying love between two people, but no relationship can long endure when built solely upon them. It is only as we learn to surrender to God, to yield our feelings, our desires, and our self-centered wishes to His will that we can exercise the type of love this text speaks of in our new relationship. As we each strive in God's strength to express His way of loving, our new marriage will prosper through the difficulties and problems we will face. Most of all, our new relationship will glorify God and reveal the awesomeness and redemptive power of God's love.

CHAPTER 8

Child Cares

There is probably no specter more horrifying to us as parents than watching our children suffer because of our actions. Even though my children were older—some of them adults—when Claire and I divorced, they felt the pain acutely. We hope the divorce will bring closure to an especially painful period of our lives and that our children will not only not suffer unduly but also somehow possibly benefit—you know, the stereotypical ending of children's stories: "happily ever after." We expect that after an initial period of struggle, our children will adjust and accept the changes that have occurred. Sadly, most don't. As parents, we often fail to understand that children experience divorce very differently than parents do.

Divorce is entirely too abstract for most children to grasp. Even within violent homes, pre-adolescent children are generally unable to make the conceptual leap needed to connect the parental behavior with the divorce. Further, most children, and even some adults, can't picture anything that is so painful working as a remedy. Children who receive painful medical treatment don't perceive it as curative. And when a parent grabs a child by the arm to prevent that child from running out into the road, the child understands only the bruised and hurting arm, not the danger from which the parent saved him or her.

So, how do we begin to understand divorce from the perspective of children? Perhaps by listening to the children themselves and trying to enter into their feelings and their grief. The problem with this, of course, is that most children are too young at the time of the divorce to articulate their feelings and concerns in a way that might be meaningful for our discussion. That is why I was so grateful to a friend who shared with me the following letters, which he wrote in reaction to his parents' impending divorce. In these words, written by a grown man, we catch a vision of the child's world of divorce. (The letters have been edited to mask the identity of those involved.)

Dear Dad,

I just wanted to drop you a quick note in reference to what is about to happen to the family. I am aware that this divorce is scheduled to be final relatively soon. However, I had hoped that the news of your first grandchild would have reminded you of the deepness of family commitments and opened the door of reconciliation between [you and Mom].

For you and Mom, there is closure—even though you both will live with the pain of this tragedy. For me, however, this problem only escalates. You know I feel you are making a terrible mistake. You need to realize that there will always be distance between us as a result of your actions. Unfortunately, I am a casualty in this war. Whoever told you I would come around after the divorce is ill-informed. I know there are those who say it is none of my business, but they are also unaware of how families react. I suggest you talk to families and children who have had their parents divorce. I have talked with over twenty in the last weeks, and each one reports terrible family separations as a result. Almost all the children, most of them now adults, say they wish they had never experienced the divorce. Even some of the divorced parents agree with that assessment.

So it is important that you are realistic about the consequences of this. To this point I have kept rather silent, but this is a tragedy for me and has hurt me more than anything that has ever happened in my life. I doubt anything aside from the death of my wife or children could be worse.

Dear Son,

It is Friday and I just picked up the mail. I don't know what else to say except I love you and am in constant pain over this. We are all casualties in a way. Our marriage failed many years ago because we couldn't seem to fix what was wrong with it. Now it is only a shell, a façade that hides the fact that it is empty inside. To continue this would be a sham and not good for Mom either. For my part, not being true to what I feel and think has made me sick. I keep rethinking this and continue talking with lots of people as to the rightness of my action. I keep coming to the same conclusion. I cannot control your relationship with me after this. That is your decision only. I will always love and be there for you no matter what.

Dear Dad,

The empty shell of the marriage you discussed is on your side only. I know Mom still has lots of feelings for you—even defends you after all you have done to her. Thus, it is you and only you who are ending this marriage. You speak of rightness, but there is no rightness in what you are about to do. You say the marriage failed because you "couldn't seem to fix what was wrong." A more true statement might be that you did not have time or emotional energy to invest in saving the marriage while it could have been salvaged. But your work was all-encompassing. You allowed this to happen [while] knowing that one of the responsibilities of a parent is to maintain the family unit and preserve the marriage.

Dear Son,

I am very hurt by the fact that you have taken sides, but all I will say is that I hope someday you will understand. We all make choices, and each of us has to decide how we will relate to each other in this new configuration of our family. The family bonds will always be there no matter what, and I believe we have to respect the love and circumstances we have shared in the past, otherwise we negate all the good there was—and there were good times.

I truly believe Mom will be happier in the long run without me because we have become so different in very important ways. There is no need to allow this to fester for the rest of our lives and our children's lives. I am not saying that there will not be hurt or that it won't be different or difficult. Of course it will hurt, but we are still a family with shared loves, and I hope we can get along and avoid misery every time someone has a wedding or a baby. This would be very hurtful and unhealthful, and I pray we can get beyond this.

Try and rid your heart of bitterness and accept us as fallible human beings who failed at their most important relationship. Learn from our mistakes and settle disagreements before they take on a life of their own and begin a destructive spiral that can't be stopped. Although you don't understand it now, we did the best we could.[1]

I hope you can see in these letters what I see: two hurt and hurting people desperately trying to get the other to see their point of view. These letters demonstrate why, in spite of our most sincere and well-meaning efforts, our communication with our children about the divorce and surrounding events often fails to achieve our aim. So, if we are to make the best of an admittedly bad situation, we'll have to reexamine our understanding of our children and how they respond. We'll also have to reevaluate our responses to them.

"Children of divorce"

There is a truism involving children of any age whose parents divorce—namely, that there is no way to overemphasize the effect parental divorce has upon them. Even twenty and thirty years later, they describe themselves spontaneously as "children of divorce." In other words, this event has become a part of these individuals' identity with perhaps even more force than does being orphaned or adopted.

Long-term studies demonstrate that children of divorce have reason to describe themselves as they do because divorce is a watershed event that dramatically alters the course of their lives in ways no one could have predicted. Children of divorce generally end up with less education than do their peers from intact families, although they usually do as well in their employment. Female children of divorce often experience sexual intimacy at younger ages than do their intact-family counterparts. And fewer of the children of divorce marry than do their peers, many of them doubt their ability to form a lasting union with a partner, and they tend to have fewer children than do those from intact families.

Because of differences in such factors as age, sex, prior family structure, and personalities, no generalizations will fit every child's reaction to divorce. However, we can say with confidence that no matter what the age, even if the "children" involved are adults, most desire their parents to have an intact marriage and no amount of reasoning will eliminate this desire, no matter how unrealistic it may be. Children view much of their early life from the perspective of their incomplete understandings of adult relationships colored by their own idealistic dreams. This is entirely normal. To a large degree, parents provide the security of their children by shielding them from most of the unsettling truths of reality. Only as the children grow older and face the hard facts of life do they come to accept the idea that things are not always as they desire. Children are prone to fantasies of a perfect world—which is the right of childhood.

So, divorce is a tragic occurrence in any child's life. Indeed, most would fare far better remaining in their dysfunctional family than in their new single-parent or blended family. However, I believe there are steps that, if prayerfully undertaken, can ease the pain and vastly improve the outcomes for children of divorce. While there is no easy, "one size fits all" solution, if we will examine children's normal development, we can gain understanding that will aid us in our task.

Divorce nearly always lessens children's feelings of security. They intuitively believe that if their parents can decide to stop loving and abandon each other, they can do the same to them. Unfortunately, our society reinforces this impression. Media—radio, music, literature, and especially television—promote the recurring theme that broken families and relationships are no big deal. Television viewing is particularly effective at conveying other negative messages that affect our children as well. Research indicates not only that children under two years old shouldn't watch television at all but also that excessive television watching throughout childhood can have adverse consequences on children's health, behaviors, educational accomplishments, and how well they prosper socially and economically. So, be wise—limit your children's television viewing.

Children, especially the very young, benefit from the structure that the family unit provides. Their lives follow predictable and, for the most part, nonvarying routines. They rise at a certain time, have breakfast, lunch, naps, dinner, bath time, story time, and bedtime. The regularity of these events shrinks their world to a size just right for their developing intellects to grasp hold of and learn from. While not every intact family is rigidly structured and, in fact, a few are downright chaotic, rarely are they totally devoid of the most basic elements of a daily schedule. And when children know what to expect and when to expect it, they feel secure.

Children develop within this structure, and as they mature, the household adapts to their ever-changing needs. For example, children find enjoyable and useful activities outside the boundaries of the home, often such things as sports, clubs, church groups, or musical instruction that involve them with other children, and the family schedule expands to include these activities. Gradually at first, but with increasing influence, friends outside the family provide both reinforcement of the children's identity as individuals and an outlet for exploration of newly maturing intellects, emotions, and interests. This is all natural and normal, as it is the way the average family adapts to the increasingly varied interests of its children by flexing and compromising on nonessentials in order to meet their needs as they move toward adulthood. Of course, the setting of limits and the occasional "No" have their place within these family dynamics.

How does divorce change these same households? It almost always alters the ability of parents to meet the needs of their children. Divorce is the most emotionally exhausting experience that adults face. Divorcing adults face massive worries over lost income, new employment, maybe returning to college, childcare issues, visitation, new adult relationships, and a host of other issues, all related in one way or another to this major life change. Most of us realize that all these problems take a toll upon our children, but we think they know we're doing the best we can under extremely difficult circumstances and that we anticipate better days ahead.

Unfortunately, children aren't likely to share this sanguine assessment of our efforts. Although they will almost never mention it, they're quite confused and fearful of the changes that are taking place. Rarely is the parent able to navigate the waters of separation and divorce while maintaining the same household routines—let alone the same routines in both parents' homes. Hence, the children must deal with home situations that are chaotic in at least one home—usually in both—and this situation may last from some months to many years. Children caught up in this situation find their mother and/or father emotionally upset or even distraught, mentally exhausted, and physically unable to cope adequately with the many demands suddenly placed upon them. Mealtimes become erratic, and because time for meal preparation suffers due to the myriad of other tasks, the quality of the meals tends to decline.

If the mom had been a full-time homemaker but suddenly must return to work, the children often don't understand the economics of the situation, only that the person they counted on is suddenly missing from their life. Both partners generally have less time for and with their children, and children of divorced families almost universally speak of the postdivorce period as an extraordinarily lonely time. Many children find their childhood suddenly ended and themselves thrown into the role of caring for younger siblings or even a parent. In many cases, no one ever really explained the divorce to the children; it was simply announced as a fact—sometimes after the fact.

Parents are caught up in their own pain. They're bearing the huge burden of caring for a single-parent household and all the while suffering the overwhelming pain of depression and loneliness. So, it's entirely human of them not even to be aware of their children's needs and to deal with them abruptly and impatiently. Consequently, not by intent, but by default, the children often feel abandoned by the ones who matter most to them. On top of this, loss of family income may require moving to a new neighborhood and a new school, and it may mean that many extras—like private school or music lesson or sports—have to be curtailed or even eliminated.

How children react

When something like a parental separation rudely interrupts children's dreams of living in a perfect world, they may react to their inner turmoil by exhibiting rebellious behavior. Or, frequently, they respond with deep, long-lasting grief. The children are emotionally hurt—hurt worse than by anything in their life before. And in many cases, they never speak of those hurts. Childish reasoning often leads them to conclude—in varying degrees—that they may have been to blame for the parents' breakup.

Of course, not all children blame themselves. The older the children, the more likely they are to blame either the father or the mother and sometimes both. Many children, perhaps most, live in a world of uncertainty, unsure of the truth about their parents' divorce. It may trouble them for years as they speculate about what caused it, yet they often don't say anything to their parents.

Why?

Studies reveal that parents rarely talk about divorce in terms children understand. Children will make judgments about who was responsible for what, and they acutely understand that no-fault divorce does not remove the basic human need for justice and moral clarity. Keep ever in mind that children quickly become experts at verbalizing what they think the adults around them want to hear. They may not verbalize their true thoughts, much less their true feelings—most children don't want to hurt or upset their parents. This is especially true when they know their thoughts and feelings will cause further alienation between Mom and Dad. Such playing to the audience is not manipulative behavior—at least not with evil intent. Rather, it is often the way children attempt to get their parents back together.

So, what should we parents do? Like it or not, we're the ones who are involved in the divorce decisions, and we must take responsibility. None of us wants to be the bad guy, to be at fault, but blame must be assessed in terms the children understand. Parents ease the burden children carry when they admit their mistakes—particularly when they do so without criticizing the other parent. We must choose our words carefully, because children often misunderstand the terms we use and don't understand the implications. We should never underestimate children's ability to misconstrue spoken language. For example, for the very young child, the words "drinking too much" are more likely to call milk to mind than alcohol. One little child thought her parents were divorcing because "they couldn't get a log."

Parents who admit to failing and who, with loving gentleness, encourage their children to grieve over the loss they have suffered encourage communication and healing. But while children will listen and even repeat the words that they aren't to blame, I must warn you that many times this doesn't mean they've abandoned the view that they are to blame. Parents will have to repeat their explanations at opportune times as the months and years pass and their children acquire greater maturity and understanding.

I fully realize that in the early stages of divorce, the last thing you feel mentally, emotionally, or spiritually able to deal with are the concerns of your children. However, the window of opportunity during which you can build on the bonds of trust may be very narrow, and your children will very quickly grasp your nonverbal signals that you aren't open to discussing their problems because you are overwhelmed with your own. Once they decide you can't help them in this crisis, they'll probably close down. Then the task of reaching their hearts again becomes much more challenging.

Divorced children are at higher risk than are children from intact families for nearly every negative influence, be it drugs, alcohol, sexual promiscuity, or other self-destructive behaviors. You can play a large role in preventing these behaviors by being actively involved in their lives. You must intentionally seek involvement if you are to really protect and shape your children's future. Unless you get to know your children intimately and learn what is going on behind the surface, little else will matter.

If you feel you lack the necessary skills for such communication, discussions with a good Christian counselor, pastor, or other single parents in your church can often provide insight, direction, and encouragement. In addition, there are a number of excellent books designed to help divorced or divorcing parents and their children to communicate—check with a Christian bookstore. I also highly recommend attending the Christian-based DivorceCare seminars. The people who produce these seminars have recently started DivorceCare seminars for children as well.[2]

The noncustodial parent

Becoming a noncustodial parent can be especially challenging, and there is no rulebook. In divorce, the lines of authority and influence become terribly skewed. For example, who sets the schedule? And when your child wants to do something with someone else on your visitation day, do you give in or insist on the visit? If you feel helplessly adrift in a sea of confusing choices, be aware that your children are even more confused. Yet you provide the key to what their long-term outcome will be. The single most significant factor in your children's success at getting through a divorce is your sincere, loving involvement in their lives.

In many cases, divorce leads children to bond with the parent whom they perceive as having been wronged or who seems weakest. Contrary to what many noncustodial parents think, children don't always do so because the other parent has poisoned the children's thoughts, although this does happen. However, children seldom can navigate the troubled waters of divorce without choosing sides. This in itself is very problematic because though they have chosen sides, their hearts are still drawn out toward the other parent in a strong bond of love and affection that, if expressed, often leaves them feeling as if they have betrayed the parent with whom they have sided. Divorce places children in the position of living a double life, of walking on eggshells trying to prevent offense, of acting one way with one parent and another way with the other.

This matter of living a double life is brutally unfair. Even young children know that it results in actions that are inherently wrong and destructive, although they don't possess the sophisticated understanding required to verbalize it. Children's comprehension is more intuitive and less reasoned, which is why some of their conclusions seem odd to adults. So, you must do everything you can to release your children from this inner stress—especially by avoiding any negative conversations about and actions toward the other parent that your children may hear or observe.

Decreasing the risks

Can you do anything to decrease the risks your children face and help them to feel secure and well-loved even after the divorce? Yes, you can. Following the suggestions listed below will help ease the difficulties.

1. Set aside time for God each day, because you need His guidance in all you do and say.
2. Spend time in intimate bonding with each of your children daily. Learn to enjoy them and give them lots of attention, affirmation, and physical reassurance in hugs.
3. Set reasonable limits and boundaries for your children. Limits and boundaries help them feel secure.
4. Offer brief prayers at mealtimes and bedtime, allowing God to be a constant, gentle, reassuring presence in their lives.
5. Pray for the other parent too. As difficult as this may be, it is vital for your children's healing process and aids them in maintaining a healthy relationship with the other parent, which they desperately need at this time.
6. Let your children know—especially by example—how important God is to you. They will notice your solid trust in God to carry you and them through this difficult time.
7. Encourage your children with the idea that because all people are members of God's family, we need to treat everyone lovingly and kindly, no matter how they treat us in return.

8. Resolve your hostilities and resentments toward your former spouse. Remember, that spouse will always be your children's parent. They can't divorce him or her.

9. Maintain as much of the pre-divorce family routine as you can. This is of tremendous value, especially for young children. If both households maintain the routine, many adjustment difficulties will be eliminated.

10. If possible, continue the primary residence for at least the short term—for example, for the rest of the school year. This too minimizes the upheaval inherent in the divorce. Parental roles may be altering, but the same home still exists, with the same school, and the same friends. Consider very carefully any relocation, especially immediately after the divorce. There are situations where it is required, but rarely do children thrive when it happens.

11. Even if not legally required, try to maintain the extras of life, such as Pathfinders or music lessons—even if it means paying more than the required child support.

12. In regard to visitation, do just what you say you will do. Visitation is a thorny issue for everyone. Understandably, in the wake of a separation or divorce, children have grounds to question our commitment. So, pay attention to keeping your word.

    Bear in mind, though, that the visitation schedule that works well for a five-year-old isn't likely to be suitable when the child is older and wants to do other activities but can't because "I have to go to my mom's [or dad's]." If both parents work together, are flexible, and get their children's input, the children will benefit greatly.

13. Pay your child support. Few other things in the relationship between former spouses raise such concern, anger, and resentment as does the failure to pay child support. Certainly, there are two sides to this issue, but I'd like to introduce to you a

third—the children's. I have rarely met any child of divorce who was unaware of the child support payment and didn't know when it wasn't paid.

Fair or not, child support is designed to help your children survive, to provide them with the basics: food, shelter, clothing, etc. It should be paid willingly and on time. It matters not what special circumstances you're in, how unfair the settlement was, etc. Failure to make those payments communicates to your children that you don't care. Sometimes the absence of a much-needed check can affect their lives quite severely. Honor God and demonstrate your love by paying child support on time.

14. However painful you might find it, attend events significant to your children even when your ex-spouse will also be there. This is very helpful for your children. You may not be able to sit with your ex-spouse during a concert in which your child is playing, but your child regards it as highly important that you both be there. It is an indication of parental unity and support. Getting together for special events, holidays, family dinners, etc., can also be helpful for your children. While doing so may fuel the fantasies they have of resurrecting the marriage, the benefit of seeing the two of you parenting cooperatively can outweigh this minor negative. Also, such cooperation markedly decreases the odds of your children trying to play one parent against the other.

15. Maintain a positive attitude while you're with your children. They quickly adopt their parents' attitudes, which determine how they will view the world around them. Rarely does anything good come from a negative attitude. Your children already have enough negatives to face; they need to be constantly exposed to a realistic, yet positive attitude.

16. If possible, don't date during the first two years following the divorce. And when you do date, avoid involving your date with

your children. It's too threatening. They reason that they've already lost one parent and now they're going to lose the other. Involve your date with your children only when marriage seems imminent.

Making the commitment

Much of what I've written in this book has discussed the merits of spending quality time with God. Your doing so is important to your children too. If you don't, who is going to model godly values of kindness, honesty, and virtue for them, and who is going to demonstrate God's nurturing character of love? Of course, this means not only spending quality time with God but also spending quality time with your children. I realize that to do this you may have to reorganize your priorities. However, I want to assure you it will be worth it. As Dr. Archibald Hart, the former dean of the graduate school of psychology at Fuller Theological Seminary, put it, "Children who have a lot of contact with both parents are the least likely to be damaged by a divorce."

Divorce doesn't end your relationship with your children, but it is up to you to maintain that relationship, because your children will rarely have the skills necessary for the task. Parenthood doesn't end when the marriage does, and while the burdens of parenthood remain and are, in fact, increased by your new marital status, the joys and privileges of parenthood also remain. It may take a while for you and your children to adjust, but joy can return to your relationships. While divorce is a tragic occurrence in the lives of our children and some may indeed carry resultant scars or insecurities into adulthood, it is within our power as adults to accept our mistakes and work with God to alter what we can.

Committing to these simple principles will be very helpful in stabilizing your spiritual life and improving your psychological well-being as well as that of your children. It will also greatly strengthen the bonds of love between you and your children and fasten them securely to the only parent who will never disappoint them—God.

Living these principles may seem very difficult at first, and you may fail often. But don't despair. God will enable you to become this kind of parent. Don't expect to be perfect; just be committed to growing in the Lord. If you have a bond of love and trust with God, your children will see it—which is one of the greatest gifts you can give them. By God's grace, it will become something they can carry with them the rest of their lives.

Remember, it is in our times of weakness and anguish that we are most likely to rely upon God. Listen to the apostle Paul: "The hardships we suffered . . . were . . . far beyond our ability to endure, so that we despaired even of life. . . . This happened that we might not rely on ourselves, but on God. . . . He will deliver us" (2 Corinthians 1:8–10). And God promises, " 'My grace is sufficient for you, for my power is made perfect in weakness' " (2 Corinthians 12:9).

Lean upon the Lord to give you love, patience, and wisdom so you may truly love and enjoy your children. Good intentions can't lead us into the best pathway for our children, nor can intellect, reasoning, or even the best of human counseling. It is only when we allow divine love and wisdom to work in us and through us that we can alleviate much of the long-term suffering our children endure because of our divorce. Remember, "His divine power has given us everything we need for life and godliness" (2 Peter 1:3). Only from the perspective of our knees will we ever gain the result we desire for our children.

---

1. For another child's perspective on divorce, see the appendix "Divorce—One Child's Story."

2. For information on DivorceCare seminars, call 1-800-489-7778 or visit these Web sites: <www.DC4K.org> and <www.divorcecare.org>.

CHAPTER 9

Forgiveness

Dying to self is giving up my rights and wishes so that Christ's love may live in me, I thought, contemplating what I had been learning over the past weeks and months. "Lord," I prayed, "this period appears to be the turning point in my life—from the past to consideration of the future. You were the One who encouraged me to check out the idea of earning a master's degree in Christian counseling, and I said I would do it if You opened the door. *Wow!* You not only opened it, You ripped it off its hinges. Now I've finished my first paper. I never thought I'd be able to do that! It's been thirty-five years since I was in an academic environment, but You helped me all the way, and it came out so well. I guess I just need to trust that when You want me to do something, You'll supply what I need to succeed. You truly are an awesome God!"

I was pleased with the changes going back to school had brought in my life. I felt that I had some purpose again—that maybe I could help others who were hurting. However, though I felt free and Claire was no longer part of my life, I couldn't seem to control my feelings about her—feelings both of love and of resentment. I still woke up with nightmares, and if I had a passing thought about the divorce, I dissolved into tears. In some areas of my life, I was finally moving forward; but in others, I seemed just as much a slave to the past as I had ever been.

As I poured out my troubles to God, He gently began to teach me what I needed to take me deeper. "Richard, the answer is in the concept of dying to self that you've been studying."

"It is?"

"Yes. Why don't we look at this logically?"

I puzzled about this, frowning slightly as I tried to see what correlation could exist between my dying to self and the residual symptoms from my failed marriage. I couldn't see any correlation unless . . . unless self was somehow linked to my feelings.

"Lord, are You saying that somehow dying to self can remove these things? I don't understand."

"How many nightmares does a dead man experience? How many times a day does he cry over the wrongs done him? Have you really died in all areas of your being, or have you just surrendered a part to Me? You see, Richard, you've allowed Me some access to your heart, but you've held on to all your hurts as if they have some value. You realize in a detached sort of way that expressing these feelings isn't healthy, so you've suppressed them. But they still wander the corridors of your mind and find expression in stray thoughts and nightmares. You can be free by surrendering these feelings to Me and dying to them. The presence of My love can dispel these thoughts and make it possible for you to forgive Claire."

"No way!" I stormed. "I can never forgive her for ending our marriage!"

"See how you cling to these negative feelings like a small child crying out, 'Mine, mine, mine!' when someone tries to take a toy away? Forgiveness is giving up your right to hate her for the wrongs she did to you. Forgiveness is evidence that you're experiencing My working fully in your life. It's your willingness to exchange the depravity of your old ways of thinking and feeling for My ways. Richard, come to Me, and I will give you rest and set you free. Don't you want to be free, really free?"

Of course I did! But it wasn't easy: The chains of the past bound me tighter than I ever imagined, until at last I realized that I had nothing to lose by letting go—nothing to lose but pain. Little by little, I began to heal as God taught me to forgive. For the first time since moving to Florida, I began to sleep through the whole night. I continued my education, began to attend group social gatherings of Christian singles, and even started to give DivorceCare seminars. My days became so active that I found less and less time to feel sorry for myself, and my episodes of depression began to diminish. God was indeed setting me free. As I moved further from my anger, it became increasingly clear that the negative feelings I had been harboring were creating a negative lens through which I filtered every event of my life. This had fueled my depression and loneliness, which in turn reinforced my anger about what I perceived Claire to have done to me and to our family.

Only as the Lord began to get through to me did I come to realize that my attitude of blaming it all on Claire was an excuse. I was playing the victim, and in so doing, I was deceiving myself into thinking I was off the hook of responsibility. But while playing the victim was comforting to my wounded pride and offended self, it was a trap that left me perpetually angry and enslaved to bitterness and resentment. Wanting to protect one's rights and to get even for the wrongs done seems so right. But God's Word says, "There is a way that seems right to a man, but in the end it leads to death" (Proverbs 14:12).

More than one kind of death

Can bearing a grudge really lead to death? Yes, it can, in a number of ways. We are more than one-dimensional creatures: We are spirit, soul, and body. When we aren't willing to forgive, we effectively block the work God wants to perform in us, and we respond to real or perceived wrongs in the sinful manner of the flesh with all its natural inclination toward selfishness. Thus, instead of forgiveness, we develop a desire for revenge. This leads us to keep track of the wrongs done to us. And focusing on the wrongs done to us creates incredible stress in our body, which can cause numerous health problems—from high blood pressure to heart disease. In extreme cases, the stress can become so overwhelming that people decide the only solution is death.

Thankfully, there is an alternative to such self-destructive behavior. We find it in forgiveness, which we can obtain by accepting the character and will of God. Listen to His attitude: "I will forgive their iniquity, and will remember their sin no more" (Jeremiah 31:34, KJV). It is this very attitude—God's attitude of forgiveness—that all of us depend upon for hope, for "we have redemption through his blood, the forgiveness of sins, in accordance with the riches of God's grace" (Ephesians 1:7). God never holds our past against us. He wants us to become like Him—not so He can have a cultlike following but because His way is what will give us true love, joy, and peace. So we are told to "Forgive as the Lord forgave you" (Colossians 3:13).

We become willing to forgive when we cooperate with the work of God's Spirit upon our hearts. We can then grant our offender forgiveness and no longer keep a record of the wrongs done to us. This relieves stress and fosters a healthy mind and body.

Paul said, "One thing I do: Forgetting what is behind and straining toward what is ahead, I press on" (Philippians 3:13, 14). I don't want to spend the rest of my life's journey looking backwards, and I don't imagine you want to do that either. If we're going to go forward with God, we must forgive. And to forgive, we need to understand exactly what forgiveness is and what it isn't.

What forgiveness is not

Because we live in a world where true forgiveness is rare, few of us understand forgiveness from a godly perspective. I've found that some of my hesitancy about extending forgiveness came from my misconceptions, so let me tell you what forgiveness is not.

1. Forgiveness doesn't mean we condone the harm done to us any more than God condones our sins when He forgives us.

2. Forgiveness isn't a sign of weakness but of commitment to the Lord and of the strength we've gained from our connection to Him.

3. Forgiveness isn't based upon feelings, because we're never going to feel like forgiving. Forgiveness is the result of a willing choice to yield to God's will because He knows what is best for us.

4. Forgiveness doesn't mean we will instantly forget. Instead, it means that we won't dwell upon what we've forgiven, and we won't bring it up again. Paul wrote that he who walks in God's love "keeps no record of wrongs" (1 Corinthians 13:5).

   However, refusing to keep a record of wrongs doesn't mean we can never identify our losses and pain. We must do that so we can know what to forgive and what mistakes not to repeat. Certainly, when we've been hurt, betrayed, or slandered, conversing with God about exactly what has happened will benefit us. It not only makes things clear in our mind, but it also helps us receive godly convictions and direction on how to handle a future relationship with the one who has wronged us. Surprisingly, a significant percentage of relationships survive infidelity, but they truly succeed only when the marriage partners undertake this type of honest assessment under God and in view of His clear expectations. However, we shouldn't take an extended period to determine our losses. Instead, we need to forgive—not so much for the other person or for our own benefit, but to please the God who loves us so dearly.

5. Forgiveness doesn't mean you necessarily trust the other person. Trust is earned and may take a long time to reestablish.

6. Forgiveness is not reconciliation. It must precede reconciliation and can lead to it, but it is a separate entity. We need to understand that our forgiveness doesn't require any action on the

part of the person who has wronged us. That person doesn't even need to ask for it before we can grant it, and it may not benefit the offending party unless he or she desires it. As we have discovered, the main beneficiary of forgiveness is the one doing the forgiving.

7. Closely related to this last point is the fact that forgiveness doesn't mean that reconciliation will automatically follow. Reconciliation depends upon the assessment mentioned above. For example, the conclusion that someone has violated your trust too badly for you to try to rebuild a relationship with that person is a decision about reconciliation. Forgiveness doesn't require us to try to rebuild the relationship. Forgiveness requires only that we yield to God's will; that, in turn, places us in the only position in which true reconciliation might be possible if the circumstances allow. But forgiveness isn't reconciliation. (We'll consider reconciliation more closely in the next chapter.)

What forgiveness is

We've looked enough at what forgiveness isn't, so perhaps it's time to consider what it is:

1. Forgiveness is my decision to walk with God.
2. Forgiveness is giving up my desire to punish the one who has hurt me. The Lord tells us, " 'It is mine to avenge; I will repay' " (Romans 12:19). This means not only that we must refrain from doing things to get back at the one who has hurt us but also that we must yield up to God the very desire for vengeance.
3. Forgiveness is real when I can sincerely wish good for the one who has wronged me. Christ taught us to " 'pray for those who persecute you' " (Matthew 5:44). Hatred always does more

harm to those doing the hating than to the ones they hate. Forgiving, on the other hand, allows God to heal our wounds and give us newness of life and purpose. And when we allow God's love to flow into and then out of our lives, it becomes a healing balm to all who have contact with us. It also frees us from the tyranny of hate. Martin Luther King, Jr., the great civil rights leader, was a man who knew what it was to be mistreated, abused, and misrepresented. Yet he said, "I am convinced that love is the most durable power in the world. It is not an expression of impractical idealism, but of practical realism. . . . To return hate for hate does nothing but intensify the existence of evils in the universe. Someone must have sense enough and religion enough to cut off the chain of hate and evil, and this can only be done through love."

4. Forgiveness of others is a nonnegotiable part of Christianity. The Lord leaves us no room for waffling about this subject. He said, " 'If you forgive men when they sin against you, your heavenly Father will also forgive you. But if you do not forgive men their sins, your Father will not forgive your sins' " (Matthew 6:14, 15).

I remember being confronted by these verses and saying, "Lord, I'm not willing! Help me to be willing to be willing." Not only did I lack the strength to forgive, I didn't even want to forgive. But God performed a mighty miracle—He helped me to be willing to forgive.

Even with my attitude change, though, I felt—in fact, I absolutely knew—that I didn't have the strength to forgive. "Of course you don't have the strength," God said. "But you aren't alone. I will be with you and supply the strength to do what you can't do on your own." I soon found myself memorizing Philippians 4:13, which assured me, "I can do everything through him who gives me strength."

5. Forgiveness is a blessed opportunity—and not for us alone, but also for our former spouse. Some people may be able to go through a divorce without saying or doing something to their spouse that they wish they hadn't, but I've yet to meet a person like that. All of us have said things that were inappropriate and even ugly. I wonder how many of us would be willing to go to a meeting where someone was going to show a video of our behavior toward our spouse during the days, weeks, or months leading up to the divorce? There's something about this process that brings out the very worst traits in all of us.

So, we must ask forgiveness, confessing the wrongs we have committed and, as much as is humanly possible, correcting them. We have an obligation to do what we can, not only to correct our wrongs but also to bring the joys of forgiveness within reach of our former partner. This doesn't mean he or she has to forgive us. Those who refuse to have anything to do with forgiveness are within their rights, and that's OK. They might not be willing even to hear our confession, and this, too, is all right. When we have done what we can, we must leave the rest in God's hands.

I know that confessing one's faults isn't a pleasant idea, because it wasn't for me. I struggled to understand the purpose behind confessing my wrongs to someone who wanted nothing to do with my religious beliefs. Eventually, though, I came to see that I was to do it to please God and to respect Claire as a child of God. You see, forgiveness is the will of God for every believer. Trusting in His will for me is the beginning of crucifying my pride, my self-will, and my fallen nature. To even consider such an action was beyond my strength, but God was there. He always meets us wherever we are. I've found that the secret for doing the impossible is to choose to do what God asks of me. If I choose to follow His will by seeking to forgive, then I receive His strength to carry out my choice. But if I choose to wait until I feel like forgiving, I will wait forever; for it is the exercise of my free will, my power of choice, that frees God to enable me.

Still, I found it terribly difficult to face the humiliation and shame of having to go to the person I saw as responsible for the divorce, confess my faults, and ask for forgiveness. It crossed my will in so many ways that I can't find the words to describe the resulting mental struggle. Eventually, however, I came across Romans 6:6, 7, 22, and as I contemplated this passage, I realized that sin is really whatever we are holding on to in place of God. So I substituted "unforgiveness" in each place where the verse said "sin," and this is what I read: "We know that our old self was crucified with Him so that unforgiveness might be done away with, that we should no longer be slaves to unforgiveness—because anyone who has died has been freed from unforgiveness. . . . But now that you have been set free from unforgiveness and have become slaves to God, the benefit you reap leads to holiness, and the result is eternal life" (adapted).

I was in shock. "You mean, Lord, that You ask me to forgive simply so I can be humbled; so that my old nature may be done away with, my self-will crucified and destroyed?"

"In a way, that is exactly what I'm doing, Richard," He said. "If you belong to Me, you are willing to allow Me to crucify your self-centered nature. 'Those who belong to Christ Jesus have crucified the sinful nature' (Galatians 5:24). You see, My dear child, true forgiveness is the product of My Spirit working in you, which allows you to experience a future in which the hurt you've experienced at the hands of someone else no longer has the final word. Even while I was being crucified, I prayed for My tormentors, asking that they be forgiven. Consequently, forgiveness, rather than sacrifice and suffering, became the triumphant theme of salvation. I want everyone to experience the healing, empowerment, and, yes, freedom that comes with forgiveness."

I didn't know if this was true. I had nothing in my experience to compare this to, so in the end, I had to step out in faith, as every child of God must when they find themselves at the crossroads of belief and action. I went to Claire and said something like this, "I am very sorry I neglected you and didn't cherish and nurture our love the way I should have for so many years. I wasn't very sensitive to your needs. Would you please forgive me for this?"

The silence was deafening. Nothing wonderful happened. Yet I had done my part. I had extended forgiveness to Claire, my former spouse. And in asking for her forgiveness, I discovered the truth of what some unknown author wrote: "When you forgive, you set a prisoner free—and only then discover that the prisoner was you!"

CHAPTER 10

Reconciliation

Lest any of you think I am approaching this subject from the perspective of the one in a million who had an easy time becoming reconciled to a former spouse, I want to inform you right now that I know how humanly difficult it is to reconcile the way God desires us to. With all our children married and fifteen hundred miles between us, Claire and I don't have a lot of contact. We are friendly when we meet or talk over the phone. However, I write as one who is continually seeking to resolve any of the residual problems my divorce left in its wake. Reconciliation is an ongoing process whenever opportunity presents itself.

Rarely is a marriage dissolved due to the isolated actions of one partner. No matter how wrongly we may feel we were treated, we've also caused our share of hurt and heartache. And while we may feel our former spouse "acts like the devil," that person is the property of the Creator, a child of God. In other words, when we sin against our former spouse, we also sin against God. So, the first step toward reconciliation is to seek forgiveness from our former spouse for our part in the situation. Then, with a clear conscience, we can come to God, who is always willing and ready to receive us with forgiveness. (See Matthew 5:23, 24.)

Remember that while attempted reconciliation has in some cases led to remarriage, it often leads to indifference or blatant rejection. Nevertheless, remarriage is what God desires—provided our ex hasn't already remarried, isn't abusive or afflicted with substance abuse, and is a believer.

People reject those they perceive as having hurt them. That's the normal human response. And in turn, when we try to reestablish friendly or even loving relationships with our former spouse and are rejected, we naturally pull back from becoming vulnerable and open in order to protect our pride or simply to prevent more hurt. This reaction also is entirely human, but it isn't God's way. He so loves us that He endures our hurt and rejection again and again in the hope that we might one day respond and be reconciled to Him. And He directs us to minister to others in the same way.

If you think such Christlike love and forgiveness for others is beyond your capacity, you are right! You and I can't do this in and of ourselves, and any attempt to accomplish this in our own strength will fail. But we have become new creatures in Christ, and the old things have passed away. When we are first reconciled to God, we choose to allow our old selves to die, and Christ raises us up in newness of life. Then we gain new desires, and we have His strength to carry out these new desires. "If anyone is in Christ, he is a new creation; the old has gone, and the new has come!" (2 Corinthians 5:17).

How does this work in a practical setting? You seek the forgiveness of your former spouse for your shortcomings, and you express your desire for reconciliation. If your spouse refuses, you can ask again as God leads you. If you are both members of the same church, you can seek the assistance of the pastor or other spiritual leaders. If both partners are willing to participate, authentic Christian counseling can be very helpful. Remember, reconciliation doesn't necessarily involve a restoration of the marriage. It does seek, at the least, to create a new working relationship with one's former spouse based upon peaceful intentions. This is vital not only for your healing, but also for your children's well-being.

Roadblocks to reconciliation

The building of a new, peaceful relationship may face a number of potential roadblocks. The most important ones are our past behavior, our current attitude toward our spouse's behavior, and our willingness to be emptied of self. When I first looked at my marriage and divorce, it was easy for me to see all of Claire's sins and faults but not so easy to examine my own. Yet who of us have traveled the pathway of separation or divorce without sinning against our former partner by slander, by using abusive language, or by expressing indifference or just plain ugliness. God says, "Your iniquities have separated you from your God; your sins have hidden his face from you, so that he will not hear" (Isaiah 59:2). No wonder many come out of divorce with a deep longing for God yet still feel a sense of separation!

God would like us to reconcile ourselves to Him by doing all we can to make amends for our offensive behaviors to those we have hurt. " 'If you are offering your gift at the altar and there remember that your brother has something against you, leave your gift there in front of the altar. First go and be reconciled to your brother; then come and offer your gift' " (Matthew 5:23, 24). The word *brother* is generic; it refers to anyone—sister, mother, friend, or coworker. It certainly includes our former partners. Further, God tells us about the other side of forgiveness. " 'If you forgive men when they sin against you, your heavenly Father will also forgive you. But if you do not forgive men their sins, your heavenly Father will not forgive your sins' " (Matthew 6:14, 15).

Solomon wrote, "He who covers over an offense promotes love, but whoever repeats the matter separates close friends" (Proverbs 17:9). These verses mean that I must not only forgive the offenses done to me, but that I am never again to bring up to anyone, especially to myself, what I have forgiven. You see, I can take the God-given gift of forgiveness and turn it from a blessing to a curse by keeping a score of how much more I have forgiven others than they have forgiven me. I can also repeatedly rehearse their faults and failings. However, in so doing, I resurrect the bitterness and hurt all over again, even while claiming I have forgiven them. I haven't really let go of my feelings of resentment.

In my own experience, God kept pointing me to I Corinthians 13:5: "[Keep] no record of wrongs." I found it hard to learn this lesson. I kept falling back into the habit of feeling sorry for myself. I decided to cooperate with God by putting another scripture into practice in my life: "Do everything without complaining or arguing, so that you may become blameless and pure, children of God" (Philippians 2:14, 15). I had to find a way to remind myself of my resolve not to bring up that which I had forgiven. So, as I noted in an earlier chapter, I started placing little notes wherever I would see them: on my desk, in my wallet, in the car, and on the kitchen counter. These notes all said "No MGC"—no moaning, groaning, and complaining.

Even as I cooperated with God to allow the miracle of forgiveness in me, I felt I would never forget. For too many of us, hurting and being hurt becomes so familiar that it seems more acceptable than risking change. This comfortableness with negative behavior also hinders our ability to forget the wrongs done to us. But God, always seeking our happiness, gently yet firmly moves us out of our old ways of thinking so He can transform us into the likeness of Christ. In time I did forget, and so will you.

The apostle Paul explained it this way: "You were taught, with regard to your former way of life, to put off your old self, which is being corrupted by its deceitful desires; to be made new in the attitude of your minds; and to put on the new self, created to be like God in true righteousness and holiness. . . . Do not let any unwholesome talk come out of your mouths, but only what is helpful for building others up according to their needs, that it may benefit those who listen. . . . Be kind and compassionate to one another, forgiving each other, just as in Christ God forgave you" (Ephesians 4:22–24, 29, 32).

You see, God understands that we sinful humans are naturally inclined to hold grudges and to work at cross-purposes with each other—especially if the one we are working with hurt or rejected us. He understands every emotional hot button to which we respond.

113

Yet, so that we may enjoy His peace, He still asks us to do the impossible in not only forgiving but also maintaining a willingness to be open and friendly even if the other party is not. This fulfills the duties of reconciliation. As is true of forgiveness, God doesn't hold us accountable for the response of the other person.

In fact, God knows our struggles, and He doesn't reject us because our hearts are "deceitful above all things and beyond cure" (Jeremiah 17:9). He knows we cannot do what He is asking, so He tells us, " ' "I will give you a new heart and put a new spirit in you; I will remove from you your heart of stone and give you a heart of flesh. And I will put my Spirit in you and move you to follow my decrees and be careful to keep my laws" ' " (Ezekiel 36:26, 27).

What an amazing God! In essence, He says, "Here is what I want you to do." We look at our hearts and our characters and say, "I can't." And He answers lovingly, "Yes, you can. I will change those things in you that prevent you from doing it." Then, if we are willing, He does in us that which we cannot do for ourselves. We may feel that we are putting forth real effort, but unseen to us, God does that which we cannot.

It reminds me of a toddler I once saw who wanted the thrill of climbing a tree like his older brother. So the toddler's father took him over to the tree and lifted him as he reached his chubby little hands up and "climbed" from limb to limb. He was putting forth effort, but his strength wasn't equal to the task. Yet his father's help took nothing away from his joy and pride at having climbed.

God's answer to my complaints

When I reached the point of beginning to try reconciliation with remarriage in mind, Claire wasn't very interested. So I wondered what the point was. I was tempted to complain, to say, "God, why did You send me out to try to reconcile when You knew it wasn't going to work? For that matter, what's been the point of all the suffering I've gone through?"

Then I read what David said, "Before I was afflicted I went astray, but now I obey your word" (Psalm 119:67). This had some truth in my life as well. I knew I had never followed God to the degree I did after my divorce, but I found that hard to admit.

I continued reading: "It was good for me to be afflicted so that I might learn your decrees" (verse 71). This was simply going way too far! Good to be afflicted? What had been so good about the things I'd gone through? After I calmed down, I thought, *Well, . . . I was learning to let God put my self to death, and I'm not so trusting of my wisdom and emotions anymore. I know these things that God has done are good, but I'm not sure they make what I have gone through worth it—or do they?*

I left my thoughts and returned to the Bible. "I know, O Lord, that your laws are righteous, and in faithfulness you have afflicted me" (verse 75). I was flabbergasted!

"God, I know You allow certain things, but this?"

"Yes, Richard, My love allows everyone freedom to choose My ways or their own. Sadly, you and Claire chose your own and consequently suffered the affliction of divorce. Nevertheless, if you stay close to Me, I will take you through your affliction and make good come out of it, even though you can't see how. Trust Me. I will get you through. I love you with an everlasting love and will not forsake you. Now listen carefully: The pathway through your valley of divorce will take you where you wouldn't have willingly chosen to go, but I will use it to draw you closer to Me than you have ever been and save you and your family."

"Save my family?" I said. "Lord, how can they ever be helped by the horror of divorce?"

I got no answer that day, so I left my conversation with the Lord unsettled. Many months later, I mentioned it to my son, and he shared something that made shivers run up and down my spine.

"I never told you, Dad, but by the time you and Mom were getting divorced, my marriage had deteriorated more than I like to admit. We were even talking about splitting up. But when we saw how badly your divorce was hurting everyone involved, we decided to try Christian counseling. It got us back on track with God and each other. We worked through our difficulties and are eternally grateful that in your grief and suffering, our marriage and family were saved. Today, our love is stronger than ever."

I was stunned and awed. God had brought good out of my horrible nightmare just as He said He would. He had parted the curtain enough for me to see that during my darkest days, when everything seemed lost, He was using my anguish for good. Once more, I was learning I could trust Him with *all* the circumstances of my life. "Lord," I prayed, "forgive me for doubting You."

In that moment of insight came another revelation. The process of reconciliation had benefited me even though I was unable to achieve remarriage with Claire. Like the dawn of a new day, it came over me that at long last I had no more bitterness, anger, and resentment. By seeking forgiveness for my faults and failures and seeking reconciliation, I had been freed! I had a closer relationship with God and more joy and peace in my life than ever before. I was now at peace with the way my life had unfolded under the guiding hand of all-wise and all-loving heavenly Father. I found I could now pray with David, "It was good for me to be afflicted." If I have learned one thing, it is to hold on to God, no matter what is happening to me.

I pray that through the passage of time and through growth in God, each of you will be able to see the good coming out of the bad. Whenever you feel discouraged over all you have lost, remember that what God promises always comes true, and He's promising you and me, " ' "I will repay you for the years the locusts have eaten . . . and you will praise the name of the Lord your God, who has worked wonders for you" ' " (Joel 2:25, 26).

Epilogue

When divorce ended my marriage, I wondered whether life would ever again hold any joy or happiness. However, step by step, God has moved in my life, sometimes dragging me—kicking and screaming!—toward a new and better existence than that which I previously knew.

Though decades had passed since I'd been involved in academic pursuits, the Lord encouraged me to return to college to earn first a master's degree and then a doctoral degree in Christian psychology. Now, as a professor at Florida Christian University, I'm engaged in the extremely satisfying work of teaching future ministers and counselors truly Christ-centered techniques for counseling the divorced and restoring marriages. I've also given more than two hundred DivorceCare® seminars, and I serve as a minister of Christian counseling and divorce care in the Forest Lake Seventh-day Adventist Church. As part of my ministry in that church, I've counseled many, especially regarding divorce and separation. So, God has blessed me with opportunities to minister to the needs of people who are struggling to overcome the effects of divorce. In so doing, He has turned my sadness into joy.

In 2003, I married a wonderful and beautiful woman named Maria. God led in our relationship, and now I again have the joy of a loving and intimate companionship. Both Maria's and my children are grown, and the arrival of grandchildren is a continual source of pleasure. Both my family and Maria's are precious to me, and I am truly blessed of God to love and enjoy them as I do.

By any measure, I've had a full life. However, though I've reached retirement age, I'm not tired. Instead, I'm continually enthused by the new life God has given me. At times during my divorce, I used to look forward to death as an end to my suffering. Now I look forward to each new day that I can spend with God, doing the work He has chosen for me.

As I move forward, the trials of life constantly remind me of the lessons I've learned in the fires of my Refiner. First, God allowed me to be in the situation I'm in today: It is His sovereign will, and I will rest in His will, trusting that He will keep me here in His love and give me all the grace necessary to bring me through. Second, I realize that times of trial can be a blessing designed to teach me the lessons God intends for me to learn. My part is to behave as His child through the grace He gives, knowing in advance that doing so may not be easy. Third, I have learned that with God, I can have inward peace and, yes, even joy, while in the midst of unhappy circumstances. And, finally, I have learned that God is going to bring me through every trial and affliction. I may not be able to see how or even know when, but He knows, so I don't have to.

My experience shows that people can overcome divorce. Through God's grace, this ultimate human tragedy can become the ultimate opportunity for intimacy and growth in our relationship with our heavenly Father. No matter where you are in your divorce experience, I want to assure you that if God can work miracles in *my* life and in the lives of the hundreds I have counseled, then surely He can work wonders in yours. Stay close to Him and trust Him always and you will experience the wonderful peace and joy that comes when the Almighty is directing your life.

I close with words that have encouraged me: "The Christian whose heart is . . . stayed upon God cannot be overcome. No evil arts can destroy his peace. All the promises of God's word, all the power of divine grace, all the resources of Jehovah, are pledged to secure his deliverance."[1] "If you go to God for help and wisdom, He will never disappoint your faith."[2]

1. Ellen G. White, *Gospel Workers* (Hagerstown, Md.: Review and Herald, 1915), 254.
2. Ibid., 418.

Divorce—One Child's Story

The following story is gut-wrenchingly sad. Unfortunately, it isn't an extreme example but rather typical. Neither of this boy's parents understood what he was going through. They probably would have been shocked if they had caught a vision of his world, of how he really felt. They probably would have said, "We didn't know." Only three little words, but they're the harbinger of much heartache when they come between your children and you.

I was eleven when my mother told me about the divorce due to my father's affair, although I had only the vaguest idea of what that was or even what a divorce was, other than the parents no longer lived together. What really hurt me most was her attitude about it—not the slightest hint of sympathy towards me. She claimed she was telling me because my father had mentioned the divorce to the neighbor and she didn't want me to hear about it from someone else. I didn't argue, but even at that age, I knew this made no sense because the neighbor in question had spoken to me maybe twice in two years. No, in my heart I sensed [that] she was telling me [in order] to get back at my father. Her behavior wasn't very nice. After all, I loved my dad.

When I got upset, she didn't even try to comfort me. Instead, she egged me on and then took great delight in calling my father at his office and reporting my response to what he had done and insisting [that] he come home and deal with me since this was all his fault! My father did come, but I got no explanation from him, only a "get over it" attitude. Then he gave me a pill—no doubt a sedative he had gotten from one of his doctor friends. I took it and that was the last thing I remembered that day. When I awoke the next morning, my father was gone and I didn't see him for some weeks.

Rapidly, I realized things were going to be different. My mother, trying to plan for the needs of her children, decided to move from the Midwest to the Southeast, where the college my sister planned to attend was located. Over that winter, I saw my father for a few hours on Sundays, and in the spring, we moved some fifteen hundred miles to a new community. My mother tried to do what she thought was best, but so many changes were hard on me. I went from being a kid in a wealthy suburb to a kid living in a tiny house in a poorer section of a Southern college town, where I knew no one and had no friends. I dressed differently, talked differently, had no supporting network, and [had] no security to draw upon.

My sister entered college, and my mother worked nights. I got up and went to school before my mother got home from work, and she was sleeping when I returned. No one pushed me to do homework, and I survived at school because I was smart, but [I didn't do] as well as I could have with just a little guidance. My new life consisted of TV—as much as ten hours a day on weekends. There was little else to do. There wasn't a single child even close to my age on the entire block.

At Christmas, my father sent a ticket for me to fly up and see him from December 28th to January 2nd. With a mixture of fear and anticipation, I took a jet—through three airports and one plane change—to see him. On the way back to his place, he told me he had been seeing a very nice woman and that he wanted me to meet her. I had hardly been in my seat long enough to warm it, hadn't seen his apartment, [and] hadn't visited with him face to face in more than six months, and my heart sank. Quickly, I felt the cold sting of resentment at having to share my father with an intruder; but of course, I couldn't say anything.

The next June he asked me to come for their wedding and family honeymoon trip, so I flew up once more. The day before the wedding we drove up to spend the night at her summer house. As the three of us settled into the loft for the night, her son Billy asked my father, "Why are you spending the night here? Why not with my mother?" Whether he was used to them sharing a bed or was just asking an honest question, I can't say.

"No," my father replied, "it wouldn't be right until after we are married."

"You will be. What difference does one day make?" Billy persisted.

"No, Billy; it still wouldn't be right," my dad answered again.

I don't believe my father ever understood the impact these words had on me. When I had visited six months earlier, Billy's mother and [my father] had spent New Year's Eve somewhere, and it seemed unlikely in separate hotel rooms. Now he was acting like a depository of virtue. Why? Just because I was there? If so, I was disgusted. He had thrown away our family to get to be with some hot little girl not much older than I was and younger than my own sister, but now he was going to pretend values he didn't believe in just to impress me? There was no discussion, no explanation. I was just left to draw my own conclusions.

This was bad enough, but I quickly concluded something worse, which was [that] for Billy's mother and her kids, my father was willing to abide by standards—at least publicly—that would protect them. That moment I felt completely betrayed. I had been replaced by people for whom he would protect the sanctity of the marriage vows—something he had refused to do for me and my family. It was at this point [that] our relationship ruptured—never to be the same. My father never understood why I never wanted to come for another visit. It wasn't talked about because, frankly, no one cared.

It has taken me decades to undo the damage wrought by my parents' divorce. My life would have been immeasurably better [if] my family had stayed in one place after the divorce, if my father had stayed involved, if I had been asked instead of told, [if I had been] given explanations rather than orders, and if I had known and experienced their love for me continually.

Seventh-day Adventist Church Standards on Divorce and Remarriage

The following paragraphs summarize material in the Seventh-day Adventist Church Manual.¹ I've included it at the request of the publisher of this book. While it applies primarily to members of the Adventist Church, it is illustrative of the fact that most denominations have policies related to divorce. You should discuss specific personal issues with your spiritual advisor.

In planning for our happiness, God intended that husband and wife should form one flesh and that their marriage should endure forever. However, humankind's fall introduced sin to this world, which has damaged God's plan for marriage.

Jesus affirmed God's original plan when He said marriage should be dissolved only when a spouse has broken the marriage vow by sexual unfaithfulness (see Matthew 5:32; 19:9). The New Testament warrants interpreting sexual unfaithfulness to include not only adultery but also other sexual irregularities, such as incest, child sexual abuse, and homosexual practices.

When marital unfaithfulness occurs, the church encourages the couple to seek reconciliation. In cases in which that cannot be attained, the church recognizes that the spouse who remained faithful to the marriage vow has a biblical right both to divorce and to remarry. However, "a spouse who has violated the marriage vow and who is divorced does not have the moral right to marry another while the spouse who has been faithful to the marriage vow still lives and remains unmarried and chaste."

The church does recognize that in some cases, marriage relations deteriorate to the point where it's advisable that husband and wife live apart from each other. It recognizes legal separation where civil jurisdictions make provision for this change in marital status. It also allows divorce where legal separation is not recognized. In both of these cases, neither spouse should remarry unless the other spouse has remarried, had sexual relations with another person, or died.

Finally, while "the church believes in the law of God; it also believes in the forgiving mercy of God. It believes that victory and salvation can as surely be found by those who have transgressed in the matter of divorce and remarriage as by those who have failed in any other of God's holy standards."

---

1. The material in this appendix is summarized from and the quotations taken from the online version of the *Seventh-day Adventist Church Manual,* <www.adventist.org/beliefs/church_manual/chapter15.html>. The manual also exists in printed form as the *Seventh-day Adventist Church Manual,* 17th ed. (Hagerstown, Md.: Review and Herald, 2005).

Recommended Reading List

In addition to the Bible, I have found the following items immensely enriching. They have touched my life over and over again.

1. Ellen G. White, *The Desire of Ages* (Nampa, Idaho: Pacific Press®, 1940). No other book has ever given me a better insight into the life of Jesus and what it means to us.

2. Watchman Nee, *The Spiritual Man* (New York: Christian Fellowship Publishers Inc., 1968). This is a most informative book regarding the relationship of our spirit, soul, and body to the Holy Spirit.

3. Ellen G. White, *Steps to Christ* (Hagerstown, Md.: Review and Herald, 1956). This little book speaks volumes regarding what the transforming presence of Christ accomplishes in us.

4. Elisabeth Elliot, *A Path Through Suffering* (Ann Arbor, Mich.: Vine Books, 1992). Suffering comes from many sources, but there is only one proven way to get through it.

5. *The Road Home—Stories of Reconciliation* (a video by Divorce-Care®; 1-800-489-7778). This excellent piece shows how people can achieve a reconciled marriage, even in "impossible" situations.

6. Hannah Hurnard, *Hinds' Feet on High Places* (Wheaton, Ill.: Tyndale House Publishers, 1979). When fear incapacitates you and you wonder where God is and why things seem to be going wrong, this allegory will answer many questions and calm your fears. (The audio book is excellent.)

7. Jim Hohnberger, with Tim and Julie Canuteson, *Escape to God* (Nampa, Idaho: Pacific Press®, 2001). This marvelous book shows real life struggles and how God's presence gives us victory.

If you enjoyed this book,
you'll enjoy these as well: